ten poems to set you free

ten

poems

to

set

you

free

ROGER
HOUSDEN

HARMONY BOOKS
NEW YORK

Published by Harmony Books, New York, New York.
Member of the Crown Publishing Group,
a division of Random House, Inc.
www.randomhouse.com

Harmony Books is a registered trademark
and the Harmony Books colophon is a trademark
of Random House, Inc.

*A complete list of credits for previously published material
appears at the end of the book.*

Printed in the United States of America

Design by Karen Minster

Library of Congress Cataloging-in-Publication Data
Housden, Roger.
Ten poems to set you free / Roger Housden.
—1st ed.
Includes bibliographical references.
1. Poetry.   2. Poetry—History and criticism.
I. Title.
PN6101.H66   2003
808.81'04—dc21   2003009179

ISBN 1-4000-5112-6

10 9 8 7 6 5 4

First Edition

FOR RAY GATCHALIAN 1946-2003

FIRE CAPTAIN, FILMMAKER, PEACE ACTIVIST,

GREAT LOVER OF LIFE AND POETRY—

ESPECIALLY THE KIND THAT FREES THE MIND.

EVER AN INSPIRATION, RAY.

"Until one is committed, there is hesitancy, the chance to draw back . . .
Whatever you do, or dream you can do, begin it.
Boldness has genius, power, and magic in it. Begin it now."
—W. H. MURRAY

Contents

Introduction

Ten poems to set you free? Free of what? Of complicated explanation, and other people's stories (Rumi); of caution and prudence (Mary Oliver); of sadness (Unamuno); of failing luck and work gone wrong (Cavafy); free of whatever it is that prevents you in this moment from claiming the life that is truly yours. It is the truth that sets you free, and these poems are its messengers.

For underlying this title is a question, one which echoes through every one of these poems: How can I stand freely in the truth of my life, feel the mettle of my unique existence, and act from there, whatever my outer circumstances may be? It is a question that has echoed down through my days. Sometimes I know what it feels like to stand in the center of my life and other times I forget. I lose myself in concerns and anxieties that have me running in circles like a gerbil in a cage. One reason I write books is to provide a structure, a context for the exploration of a question that absorbs me; and no question has taken up more of my attention than this one. In fact, the question itself has often had me chasing my tail.

When I have not known what to do with myself or where to turn next in my life, my deepest consolation has been to spend some time in solitude. There, I am usually able to return to myself. In times like this, my companion is likely to be a book of poetry. Unlike prose, poetry does not explain things. It conveys the *feeling* of what happens. It articulates our deepest wonderings and aspirations, it shows us the world and ourselves in ways we might never have noticed before; it can name the questions that we wrestle with. Sometimes, it can prompt you to live your own answers in response. All of the ten poems in this book have done this for me. The essays that follow them are a response to the poems from my own life experience.

Poetry, like anything else, is no miracle cure, no quick formula that you can apply to kick-start your life into action and fulfillment. Nor are the essays that follow the poems. But good poetry emerges from the wellsprings of the human spirit, and if we are in the right place in ourselves to hear it, it can call forth our own inarticulate knowings, and offer a mirror into the core and the truth of our own life. It can show us the spark, the fire at our center, which, in the end, is the only thing in us likely to endure, the one thing worthy of our true name. That fire is the real life in us, and it is this, in their different ways, that the poems in this little book invite us to claim.

The book is little because there is no need to overstate its case. These ten great poems are more than enough to send a shudder through your bones and remind you who you are and can be (for that is the real question). More than enough, too, to help you feel without fear the emptiness that can well up when you are faced with the big canvas of life, and, seemingly, no paintbrush.

What a short span we are here for, in this tender body of nerve and sinew, flesh and blood! Better then, to shape our experience with insights that mirror our deeper being, rather than with the passing flotsam of doubts and anxieties, hopes and fears, that can so easily fill the screen of our mind. These poems, in their different ways, speak from the store of human wisdom and insight, which shall always survive both the trials of time and the persistent opacity of our collective darkness.

Shake off this sadness, and recover your spirit

the poem by Miguel de Unamuno begins. Unamuno's message is a call to action, and when it comes to kindling the fire in your life, action is often, though not always, what is needed. Remember those lines by Mary Oliver that begin her poem "The Journey":

> *One day you finally knew*
> *what you had to do, and began, . . .*[1]

It is one thing to know what you have to do; it is another to actually begin doing it. Both Oliver in "The Journey" and Unamuno in "Throw Yourself Like Seed" urge us to make that tiny, momentous step along the road that is ours to tread. I know from experience that one can easily fritter away months and even years talking, thinking, dreaming about what one may or may not do, instead of taking that first small step that is willing to exchange the safety of talk for the thrill and the risk of action. The kind of action that Unamuno means is specifically that of work:

start then, turn to the work

he says later in the poem. For

> *from your work you will be able one day to*
> *gather yourself.*

Work—what kind of work will fulfill us, be the vehicle for our creative energies, make a difference, provide a good income—is probably the single greatest challenge that most of us share, along with the task of intimate relationship (or the flip side, getting along on your own). Unamuno doesn't know what is best for you—nobody does—but his powerful words may be just the nudge you need to tip you over the edge into the fullness of a life that has been waiting for you all along. You never know. Try it. Read it. Not once, or twice, but several times over a week or so. And read it out loud to yourself, and slowly, so the meanings and the layers of the lines seep into you, and reach a place below your critical faculties. Read it to your lover, or to a friend, and have him or her read it back to you.

Do the same with all of these poems, for they deserve your

care and attention. They are the fruit of the deep mind, of luminous insight, and they can call forth the same in you if you enter them this way.

> *And who will care, who will chide you if you wander away*
> *from wherever you are, to look for your soul?*

Mary Oliver asks, in her poem in this collection. For to live your true life is not just a matter of asserting your personal will in the world. It is not dependent on your level of outer ambition and worldly success, though these may indeed be an expression of the underground flare that your true life comes from. No, the life we are speaking of here cannot be gauged by where you are on the career ladder, or by how much money you have in the bank. As Mary Oliver reminds us in the lines above, we are speaking of the life of the soul. And that life can be felt when you stand without excuse or apology in the outer world by the deepest truth you know inside.

This is why the theme of authenticity whispers its way through many of these poems, as in David Whyte's "Self-Portrait," in which he says he wants to know

> *if you are prepared to live in the world*
> *with its harsh need*
> *to change you. If you can look back*
> *with firm eyes*
> *saying this is where I stand.*

And as Rumi, who in Coleman Barks's version called "Unfold Your Own Myth," says:

> *But don't be satisfied with stories, how things*
> *have gone with others. Unfold*
> *your own myth, without complicated explanation, . . .*

Then Stanley Kunitz, who says, in "The Layers":

> *I have walked through many lives,*
> *some of them my own,*
> *and I am not who I was,*
> *though some principle of being*
> *abides, from which I struggle*
> *not to stray.*

Jane Hirshfield's poem, "Lake and Maple," takes a different though related turn, by speaking to the need, the longing, to be fully engaged, utterly given to the life that is ours:

> *I want to give myself*
> *utterly*
> *as this maple*
> *that burned and burned*
> *for three days without stinting*
> *and then in two more*
> *dropped off every leaf; . . .*

Who has not felt that longing to give oneself utterly—to a piece of work, perhaps, to the swell and movement of our own life, even to something we may have no name for? Mary Oliver, in her poem here ("Have You Ever Tried to Enter the Long Black Branches?") has her own ecstatic way of calling us to this degree of devotion:

For how long will you continue to listen to those dark shouters, caution and prudence?

Fall in! Fall in!

This is the third book in the Ten Poems series, and there is a Mary Oliver poem in each volume. Rumi's voice, too, is in each of the books. Both these poets, separated by seven hundred years, cry out in their own ways for an ecstatic immersion in life. Both are poets of love and truth, and I believe that no time more than our own has been in such need of their fierce, uncompromising calls, calls for love and truth that cut clean and straight to the bone. That is why I return to them again and again.

Do you think this world is only an entertainment for you?
. . . .
No wonder we hear, in your mournful voice, the complaint that something is missing from your life!

Mary Oliver's ecstasy comes laced with a sober, astringent clarity into the nature of the human condition. In her poem "So Much Happiness," Naomi Shihab Nye, on the other hand, calls us to our true estate by reminding us that, in essence, happiness is who we are. It is a natural result of claiming the life that is ours. Yet there is no effort in this claiming; no striving to get things right, to be at the helm of one's life like a captain in a storm. It is rather a saying Yes! to what is already so. To who we already are. What is happening when you are happy is *you:*

> *you shrug, you raise your hands, and it flows out of you into everything you touch. You are not responsible.*

Anna Swir, in her poem "Thank You, My Fate," makes something of the same discovery while making love. In his poem "The God Abandons Antony," the Greek C. P. Cavafy adds another layer of meaning to a life fully lived. He urges us, along with the poem's protagonist, Mark Antony, to embrace the losses in our life along with everything else. For they, too, are part of who we are; they, too, play their part in the process of our soul-making.

I had a fuller understanding of what he meant only recently, when I returned after some time to my origins, in England. I took in the land, the buildings, the frail light of the place, and felt how profoundly they nourished me. I felt, too, how likely it was that I would never live there again, having settled now in America. For the first time, I felt the full loss of my native country. Cavafy's poem helped me not to minimize the truth of what I was leaving behind, not to play it down or rationalize it away, but rather to stand there and take in the full weight of it for what it was. I was claiming my origins in the same moment as leaving them.

Finally, the monk and writer Thomas Merton, in his poem "In Silence," asks us directly the question that is implicit in all of these poems:

> *Who are you?*
> *Who*
> *Are you? Whose*
> *Silence are you?*

He asks if we dare sit in the silence and risk everything we know dissolving into thin air. We are not, after all, who we think we are. *Who* you are, any one of these poems might just be the door to. As could the view through your window, the silence in the room when you wake up in the morning, the look on the cashier's face as you buy this book, or another. You never know. But why not start, turn the page, and find out?

1

SELF-PORTRAIT

by David Whyte

*It doesn't interest me if there is one God
or many gods.
I want to know if you belong or feel
abandoned.
If you know despair or can see it in others.
I want to know
if you are prepared to live in the world
with its harsh need
to change you. If you can look back
with firm eyes
saying this is where I stand. I want to know
if you know
how to melt into that fierce heat of living
falling toward
the center of your longing. I want to know
if you are willing
to live, day by day, with the consequence of love*

and the bitter
unwanted passion of your sure defeat.

I have heard, in that fierce embrace, even
the gods speak of God.

Look in the Mirror

"Self-Portrait" is a poem David Whyte wrote after looking in the mirror one morning. I don't know what kind of morning it was for him, but I suspect that things in his life were coming to some kind of head, that something was calling him to stand up, wake up, and be honest about what his life was needing him to be and do. And yet, so much of Whyte's poetry has this wakening call. His is a voice that will always champion the truth of the soul over the clamor of the social personality.

What do *we* see when we stumble out of bed in the morning and gaze in the mirror? What do those lines, those eyes—the way we hold our head—our familiar face reflect to us of the heart and soul of our life? What does it say about what matters to us, about how open we are to the questions in our hearts? Or is our image shaped instead by a mask of acquired and inflexible opinions?

Whyte's poem starts with a fierce declaration, that he has no interest in whether there is one god or many gods—in what opinions his personality may or may not have acquired over time. Religious and philosophical positions are irrelevant when we gaze into the truth of our life. Confronted with ourselves in the mirror, what we might see, if we are willing to look, are the feelings that run deep in our veins and leave their mark in our eyes, in the set of our jaw, on our every word and gesture.

Consider your own responses to the questions Whyte asks in this poem. They are not, after all, the kind of thing you might be asked at a dinner party. When someone asks about us, we are more likely to reel off a litany of the things we do, or have, or believe: I'm an artist, a Christian, a Buddhist. I am poor. I am rich, with a fine career. I am against the warmongering of powerful nations, against the ruination of the environment, and I love poetry, Mozart, and weekend trekking. You know, the kind of thing you see every week in the lonely-hearts columns. But this is merely the skin of who we are.

Our deeper feelings run in the blood. How would you respond to Whyte's first question? Do you feel you belong? My own response is both yes and no. I live in a country, the United States, which I moved to just a few years ago. Culturally and historically, then, I am an outsider. Even when I lived in my native England, I still felt on the margins of the mainstream culture around me. As a writer, I have rarely had a job or career that slotted me securely into the daily work patterns of the majority. I was born illegitimate, which, in postwar England, singled me out. I have spent my life traveling to distant places in response to the persistent itch that has pursued me, until recently, for most of my days.

The only places I have belonged—where I have felt entirely at home in my own skin—are those places, both in the landscapes of the world and those of the heart, where I have loved. I have loved and been loved in intimate relationships.

I have known an abiding love for certain natural settings—the hills and valleys around the city of Bath, in England, where I grew up; the craggy rocks and nestled villages of Provence, where I have spent as much time in my imagination as I have in fact. I have also loved and felt loved in the deep silence I have known to lie beneath all thinking and feeling. This last belonging—the belonging in presence—is, in my experience, the one that survives all. Its echo lingers even in the thickest of the many dark woods in which I have sometimes lost my way.

The theme of belonging, by the way, is a defining note, a constant through all of Whyte's work. In "Sweet Darkness," he urges us to

> *Give up all the other worlds*
> *except the one to which you belong.*[1]

In "What I Must Tell Myself," he says that

> *When you are alone*
> *you must do anything*
> *to believe*
> *and when you are*
> *abandoned*
> *you must speak*
> *with everything*
> *you know*
> *and everything you are*
> *in order*
> *to belong.*[2]

And yes, I have also felt abandoned at times—by the fates; in an early love, briefly; and as a child outside the babysitter's door. More often, though, my life has been a creative tension between a condition of longing and one of belonging. The longing is something different to the feeling of abandonment. One longs for something only when one feels it to be close, or at least attainable. Abandonment is a condition of helplessness. Perhaps the value of abandonment as an adult is this, its capacity to break our shell of self-sufficiency, and also our hopes of being rescued by someone else. When our dreams lie scattered about us, we may cry out in the truest voice we have. When that dark deep voice cries out unrestrained in its utter aloneness, it can bring down the heavens above.

All this, the true mirror reveals. Just as it will tell the truth about our despair; our hopelessness; whether we wear it with courage on our face, or whether we are still holding it at bay with a (cracked but) cheerful smile, with hopeful affirmations, or with some esoteric spiritual practice. If we have not known despair—if we have not felt the weight of it in our body and mind—we have yet to join the great majority of the human race. Our face will not bear the marks of that maturation.

I do not think that Whyte is raising one experience above another here. He is not interested in whether the feeling of belonging is a better place to be than feeling abandonment or despair. That is not the point. What matters, he seems to be saying, is that you be honest with your own experience; that you name it, take it on as your true estate in this moment.

That, more than any job description or set of opinions, is closer to who you are. Then, speaking as ever to us as well as to himself, he asks if you are

> *prepared to live in the world*
> *with its harsh need*
> *to change you.*

I read *world* as this human family we are born into. Who, among those who have tried to discover their own unique path, has not felt the gravitational pull of parents, family, the corporation, the culture at large, drawing them back to the consensual norm? The human matrix we are born into tries to preserve itself that way, by dissuading us from being different. Our challenge is to be able to bend like the willow in the wind—for great winds there will always be—and return to our original shape.

Only we can know what it is like from the inside to be on our particular journey, and there will always be times when the world in its various guises tries to make us go its way rather than our own. Our individuality, our true sense of self, grows to the degree that we are able to hold fast to what we know to be true for ourselves, even when others are crying out for us to follow more well trodden paths. Robert Frost, in his famous poem "The Road Not Taken," knew this well:

> *Two roads diverged in a wood, and I—*
> *I took the one less traveled by . . .*[3]

And that, writes Frost, is what made all the difference. The whole theme of Whyte's poem, then, is authenticity. What matters is that

> *you can look back*
> *with firm eyes*
> *saying this is where I stand.*

Whyte's *firm eyes* are a reflection of Stanley Kunitz's *principle of being / that doesn't change,* as he calls it in "The Layers." The most durable form of integrity, Whyte says, requires more than naming your deepest feelings and standing by them. It requires falling headlong into the desire that lies in your heart of hearts, whatever name you give it. If you can melt into *that* fire, your days will be shot through with *a fierce heat of living,* no matter how small or mundane your outer activities may seem.

The next few lines of Whyte's poem make me shudder. They cut to the quick. See what happens when you do what he did. Look into the mirror and ask yourself the question:

> *I want to know*
> *if you are willing*
> *to live, day by day, with the consequence of love*
> *and the bitter*
> *unwanted passion of your sure defeat.*

What would *you* consider the consequence of love to be? I would say that love calls us to give ourselves utterly, to fall without reserve toward the object of our love, whether it be the inner flame of our own existence, or some outer love in the form of another person. *Love asks us to offer up our heart for breaking.* In short, it seems to ask the impossible. Love certainly seemed to be asking the impossible of me when I fell in love with a woman with three children. I thought I had moved on from the householder stage of life. These last few years, and despite my protestations, love has been ruthlessly whittling away my objections.

I would like to think that in these lines Whyte is urging a day-by-day commitment to that love without any holding back, a daily return to what we knew in a first moment of inspiration and recognition. Even if, today, the fire seems to have gone out, can we still live from that original knowing?

The consequence of a call such as this is certain to be our "sure defeat." We can only respond to love with all that we are, which includes our frailties and shortcomings. All of us, as human beings, are inherently flawed. Perhaps this is another layer of meaning here, that the call of love for our absolute surrender is in itself impossible to sustain day by day, moment by moment.

The ego, the personal identity that is constructed around our own needs and wants and fears, is always defeated by love in any event. The ego is incapable of loving. Only when some other identity emerges in us, one with *firm eyes*, can love begin to seep through the cracks of our life. But then, apart from our daily fears and failures, there will always be death, which will scatter our dreams and our loves like dust in a strong wind.

Yet the whole point is not, in the end, a matter of succeeding or failing. It is a matter of putting one's head on the chopping block of life and taking what comes. Of being willing to love even though love is bound to defeat us finally, if not through loss, if not through separation, then certainly in death. I am reminded, too, of the poem "The Man Watching" by Rilke, a poet whose work has inspired and informed that of David Whyte. The poem speaks of a man who has no interest in winning:

> *This is how he grows: by being defeated, decisively,*
> *by constantly greater beings.*[4]

We are defeated by fate; we are defeated, too, by love, if we ever find ourselves in that perilous arena; and we are always and ever defeated by death. We will be slowly or quickly broken on the wheel of time. Even as we are being dismembered, can we stand by our heart's deepest love? The question is not intended to rouse our will, for it is not our will that is done in affairs like these. This kind of falling is nothing less than grace.

> *I have heard, in that fierce embrace, even*
> *the gods speak of God.*

When a man or a woman has the grace and the privilege of falling into the love at the center of their being—into the human heart's mysterious willingness to love in the face of inevitable defeat—then, even the gods themselves bow down.

2

LAKE AND MAPLE

by Jane Hirshfield

I want to give myself
utterly
as this maple
that burned and burned
for three days without stinting
and then in two more
dropped off every leaf;
as this lake that,
no matter what comes
to its green-blue depths,
both takes and returns it.
In the still heart,
that refuses nothing,
the world is twice-born—
two earths wheeling,
two heavens,
two egrets reaching
down into subtraction;

even the fish
for an instant doubled,
before it is gone.
I want the fish.
I want the losing it all
when it rains and I want
the returning transparence.
I want the place
by the edge-flowers where
the shallow sand is deceptive,
where whatever
steps in must plunge,
and I want that plunging.
I want the ones
who come in secret to drink
only in early darkness,
and I want the ones
who are swallowed.
I want the way
the water sees without eyes,
hears without ears,
shivers without will or fear
at the gentlest touch.
I want the way it

accepts the cold moonlight
and lets it pass,
the way it lets
all of it pass
without judgment or comment.
There is a lake,
Lalla Ded sang, no larger
than one seed of mustard,
that all things return to.
O heart, if you
will not, cannot, give me the lake,
then give me the song.

Give Yourself Utterly

I want to give myself
utterly
as this maple
that burned and burned
for three days without stinting
and then in two more
dropped off every leaf;

This beautiful poem is nothing less than a prayer. Sometimes
when I go to bed at night and can't sleep, these first few lines
surface from the lake of my mind and still all the ripples.
Their sonorous beauty rings deep in my bones. They have
become one of those thought-images for me that Yeats was
referring to when he said:

> *He that sings a lasting song*
> *Thinks in a marrow bone.*[1]

Most of our thoughts circle in the mind alone, but a few
reach down deep and become part of who we are. This is
one such image for me, and it has become a lasting source of

nurture and consolation. The ease with which the maple gives itself over to burning—to its leaves reddening deeper and deeper—and the simplicity with which it lets those same leaves fall, is a reminder to me that a life fully, entirely lived is not necessarily one that needs to rely upon the struggle of the individual will to fulfill its ambitions.

Surely most of us have longed to feel so engaged, so entirely given over to life, that every last drop of us is fully used up. Yet the images we have in our culture for giving ourselves over—whether to a religious devotion, an artistic endeavor, or some social cause—are mostly fanatical ones of people possessed. History is full of larger-than-life characters striding across the world stage with steam pouring out of their ears and sometimes a masterpiece or two, or even many, appearing from their gargantuan energy and creativity. Think of Beethoven, Mozart, the fury of a Picasso or a Jackson Pollock, not to mention Dylan Thomas, Ezra Pound, or shooting stars like Virginia Woolf. It is a sobering fact that a large proportion of creative people in general "burn out," and even self-destruct, on an obsessive energy that, at different times in history, has been considered synonymous with creativity.

Is it necessary, though, to burn like a fuse wire in order to be given utterly to life? Do you have to go down in a fury of drugs or alcohol, commit suicide, or die, like so many nineteenth-century novelists, of syphilis in order to know you have lived life to the full? I don't think so. The passion that Jane Hirshfield is speaking to in this extraordinary poem emerges from a quite different level of experience. She is talking about giving herself over, not to a particular task or project, but to the whole movement of life itself, as it moves through *her,* whatever form it takes.

The crescendo of desire—*I want, I want*—that ripples through every line of this poem stems from a deeper, altogether quieter stream. The image itself of the maple is one of beauty and grace, of nature and quiet. And the way a tree drops its leaves is effortless, without struggle or torment of any kind. The tree knows, with Mary Oliver, that

> *what's coming next*
> *is coming with its own heave and grace.*[2]

No need, then, to force any issue. Leaves will fall in their own time, nothing can hold them back; knowing that, you will naturally be willing to let every last one go. In a line from another glorious poem of hers, "Ripeness," Hirshfield says that

> *Ripeness is*
> *what falls away with ease.*[3]

We become ripe—we reach our true maturity—when we can have the grace of the maple, and let things both come and fall away from our lives in their season—a relationship, perhaps, or a form of work, but above all, a new or an outworn idea of who we think we are.

This is not to say that we coast along in neutral through life and take what comes with a philosophical shrug. That is no way to live from the core of your life; nor is it the tenor of this poem. No, what Jane Hirshfield wants here is nothing less than union with all life through the falling away of the sense of a separate self. This kind of wanting is the most ardent of all. That's why the poem has the feel of a prayer— she is sending her wish out on the breath, as if enjoining the larger life to hear her and lend its greater energy—its grace—to her wish. Language of this sort may be a little too Christian in flavor for Jane Hirshfield's taste, for she is a Buddhist, and spent several of her younger years in a Zen monastery. And yet Christian and Buddhist are one in their acknowledgment that

> *In the still heart,*
> *that refuses nothing,*
> *the world is twice-born—*

This is the heart of the poem for me.

> *Be still and know that I am God*

it says in the Bible.[4] When the lake of the mind is without a ripple, we are born again in the spirit, for in that silence the ego awareness falls away. "Rest in natural great peace, this exhausted mind," the great Tibetan Buddhist master, Dudjom Rinpoche, used to say. The world over, the same message. And here, in the lines of this poem, we are shown the quality of that stillness—nothing is refused there. Everything is allowed to rest, to be as it is; not out of indifference, but out of a deep, passionate acceptance of life as it is in this moment. All the other images in the poem serve to emphasize and draw out this insight.

Hirshfield wrote this poem at Yaddo, the writers' retreat, inspired by the lake and the maple tree there. She saw how the placid waters held a reflection of the earth above, the sky, the egret, and even, for an instant, a fish. In the lake's stillness, there are two of everything, the world is twice-born, as it is in the still heart. But what I love is this: She is not merely wanting some disembodied state in which she can remain unmoved and untouched by life. No,

> *I want the losing it all*
> *when it rains and I want*
> *the returning transparence.*

Bring it all on, she is crying; hold nothing back. Let me know what it is like to lose everything—even the stillness, the composure, the clear reflection, all of it—let it pour with rain so the lake's surface (the mind's surface) is shaken and muddied. Let that happen, because that is what happens here on earth to human beings. But let the *transparence* return in its due time, and the whole cycle begin again, and again; for the ebb and the flow is everything.

The stillness she wants is not stasis; it's not antilife; it is an intimation of something that encompasses all opposites, all ebbs and flows. Ultimately, it is not a condition at all; it is the ground of everything that is, including your own mind. And this kind of ground cannot be shaken by any conditions.

This, I think, is the undercurrent that runs through the poem.

I want, I want, the wanting is mounting as the poem moves on. Have you known such a longing as this? Can you recognize the long, passionate, poem-length cry of life to Life? It reminds me of those lines of Rumi:

> *There is a passion in me that doesn't long*
> *For anything from another human being.*[5]

I recognize Jane's longing, and I know how much of the time my own life seems to fall short of such quiet intensity. Most of my days are spent just bumbling along. I often have no idea what I am meant to be doing or why I am here. I can spend hours in any given week wondering if I am living in the right place, if I am using my time to best effect, or feeling the emptiness that food won't fill. But perhaps that is also what she means when she says she wants *the losing it all / when it rains.* The emptiness, the ambivalence, is all part of it. Part of life, that is. My life. Bring it all on. Let it all be part of the great dish I am served, part of all *that plunging* and swallowing the poet herself wants a few lines on.

This whole poem is a call to become not less, but more moved by life, and in all of its guises, rain or shine. Hirshfield wants to be like the water that

> *shivers without will or fear*
> *at the gentlest touch.*

When my daily anxieties and strivings fall away, I am even more likely to shiver in response to a gentle touch because I am less defended, more open to the subtle currents of feeling and sensation that would normally pass me by. I am more like the maple, whose leaves tremble with every breath of air.

The light of the moon can pass through me, I can feel its passage, and have no need for *judgment or comment.* Imagine what that would be like, to live a day, an entire day, without any judgment or comment. I suspect we might not have a great deal to say; certainly our minds would be far quieter than usual.

> *Don't keep searching for the truth;*
> *just let go of your opinions. . . .*

said Seng-ts'an, the Third Zen Patriarch of China.[6]

In the last few lines Jane Hirshfield sends out one last great cry. Lalla Ded was a legendary female saint, a wandering yogini in India several hundred years ago. The lake she sang of in her songs, no bigger than a mustard seed, lies deep in the human heart. If she cannot know that lake directly for herself, Hirshfield says, then at least, let her heart be filled with the song of it. Let her faith in its existence sing out in praise. For our song is the echo, the return message, of what we seek. "Rest in natural great peace," Dudjom Rinpoche said. May we long for that peace with all our hearts. That wish, that song is, itself, the most precious gift.

3

THROW YOURSELF LIKE SEED

by Miguel de Unamuno

Shake off this sadness, and recover your spirit;
sluggish you will never see the wheel of fate
that brushes your heel as it turns going by,
the man who wants to live is the man in whom life
is abundant.

Now you are only giving food to that final pain
which is slowly winding you in the nets of death,
but to live is to work, and the only thing
which lasts
is the work; start then, turn to the work.

Throw yourself like seed as you walk, and into your
own field,
don't turn your face for that would be to turn it
to death,
and do not let the past weigh down your motion.

Leave what's alive in the furrow, what's dead
in yourself,
for life does not move in the same way as a group
of clouds;
from your work you will be able one day to
gather yourself.

Recover Your Spirit

When the fascist General Milan-Astray stormed into the University of Salamanca to confront the elderly professor and poet-philosopher Miguel de Unamuno over his criticism of Franco and the fascist cause, Unamuno said to him:

> At times to be silent is to lie. You will win because you have enough brute force. But you will not convince. For to convince you need to persuade. And in order to persuade you would need what you lack: reason and right.

The general shouted, "Death to intelligence! Long live death!" and drove the ailing poet out of the university at gunpoint. The poet suffered a heart attack and died within the week. It was 1936, soon after the outbreak of the Spanish Civil War.

Unamuno's name is remembered in Spain, even today, as a symbol of courage and integrity. And here we are now, contemplating his poetic legacy, while the name of the general has long since fallen into obscurity. Two thousand years or more before the general confronted Unamuno, Euripides said:

> When good men die, their goodness does not per-
> ish but lives, though they are gone. As for the bad,
> all that was theirs dies and is buried with them.[1]

History has challenged Euripides' statement time and again, but even so, the spirit of it stands, and certainly in the case of Unamuno. Although Lorca, his younger contemporary (who was also murdered by Franco's forces), is better known internationally today, Unamuno is still acknowledged in Spain as one of the great thinkers and poets of the last century.

> *Shake off this sadness, and recover your spirit;*

The first line of this rousing poem reminds me of those lines by Mary Oliver in her poem "Wild Geese":

> *Tell me about despair, yours, and I will tell you mine.*
> *Meanwhile, the world goes on.*[2]

But while Oliver is urging us to turn our eyes from our troubles to the bigger view that nature offers, Unamuno is counseling action, and specifically, work. Have you ever heaved your body through the day with the feeling that nothing is really worth the effort? That your own sadness, loneliness, or confusion weigh so heavily on your shoulders that you have neither the space nor the inclination to look up and see anything else? I have. Sometimes, those days can oblige a necessary pause in what may seem to be an endless cycle of busy-ness. Days of sadness can have their value. But I think it is the self-absorption that Unamuno is pointing to, the indulgence in our troubles that makes our whole being feel *sluggish*.

> *sluggish you will never see the wheel of fate*
> *that brushes your heel as it turns going by,*

This kind of lethargy, or dullness of spirit, can cause us to miss not only opportunities, but even the whole direction and purpose of our life. We forget what we are here for, and don't even notice when the door opens in front of us—the very door we may have been anticipating all of our life.

To indulge ourselves in this way, Unamuno says, is to give food

> *to that final pain*
> *which is slowly winding you in the nets of death,*

Perhaps *that final pain* refers to death itself, which can eat into us by means of the corrosions of despair and depression. I wonder what these lines mean for you. For me, *that final pain* might also refer to a life not fully lived, one that has been shrouded in regrets over what might have been, or what wasn't. The pain is *final* because it is all we are left with at the end of a life in which we have never dared to nurture our own flame.

> *but to live is to work, and the only thing*
> *which lasts*
> *is the work; start then, turn to the work.*

Remember Rilke, who said, speaking to God in one of his poems,

> *But what you love to see are faces*
> *That do work and feel thirst.*[3]

Rilke suggests here that work is the greatest offering we can make to Life, God, call it what you will. In work, we, too, become creators, and act in the likeness of the Intelligence that made us. Rilke's tutor in this was the great French sculptor Rodin, for whom Rilke worked as a secretary for a time. Rodin would always tell the young, sensitive poet that the essential thing for an artist was not dreaming, or talking, but work. *"Travailler, travailler, travailler,"* Rodin shouted once, trying to explain how new works came to him.

In saying that *to live is to work*, Unamuno even infers that a life without work is itself a kind of living death. But the work that is truly yours is the life that is truly yours; and if we have created something from our labors, it will speak for us long after we are gone.

Neither Unamuno nor Rodin nor Rilke was speaking out of some culturally ingrained Protestant work ethic. They were not concerned with being "useful." No, they were passionate about doing what they had come here to do; and they all knew, in their own way, the crucial value of dedication and commitment to their chosen vocation.

The next line is the key to the work Unamuno is referring to:

> *Throw yourself like seed as you walk, and into your*
> *own field,*

Give yourself away, he urges, and to what will ultimately be your own will and testament—dedicate yourself to your own talents, whatever they may be. Give everything you have— body, mind, and soul—to that endeavor. At the same time, the image of throwing yourself away implies less an effort than a self-offering, a complete surrender to what is required—as if the work were bigger than you are. If you do not do this, the poem goes on to warn, you will be inviting death. You must shake off your doubts, take up your bed and walk, and without looking back. It is never too late to live the life that is yours.

That's all very well for a Rodin or a Rilke, you may say, but many of us—most of us—do not know what our true work is. Like me, you may have spent much of your lifetime with the nagging feeling that you are not quite doing what you came here to do. Or perhaps you feel an outsider, somehow, to the mainstream current of fashions and events, someone whose gifts do not fit easily into the prevailing culture. We need to cherish these feelings, and look into them deeply.

The pain they can cause us may be due less to their message than to our interpretation of it.

Instead of concluding that these feelings make the life we are leading seem wrong in some way, we can look for the value they bring to our lives. Outsider status, for example, can be a privileged, if sometimes painful, position to have. For the price of feeling lonely, and, often, unheard, it can offer a unique perspective that can be known in no other way. Every artist, every visionary in any field, must be willing to pay that price. Unamuno urges us to persist in what we know, in what we imagine to be possible, regardless of the cost. You persist by putting one foot in front of the other,

> *as you walk, and into your*
> *own field,*

If you want to know what you are here to do, look around you, at the life you already have. It will tell you what to do next if you follow the deepest thing you feel inside. You may realize that, ultimately, your own true vocation has no outer form; that your dedication is to an inner life that is not concerned with the work you do. What matters, finally, is less what it looks like—the presence or absence of a string of achievements—than the pouring of your heart and soul into the longings and loves you have been given.

> *Leave what's alive in the furrow, what's dead*
> *in yourself,*

Unamuno's images of seeds and furrows are an echo of the passage in the Gospel of John (12:24) where Jesus says,

> Truly, I say unto you, unless a grain of wheat falls into the earth and dies, it remains alone; but if it dies, it bears much fruit.

There is a form of dying that is necessary when you give yourself utterly to your work—whether it be raising children, writing novels, tending a garden, or caring for the sick. Our work calls us—our life calls us—to surrender our smaller selves to the greater task. If we do not submit to that process, we shall remain outside the stream of life, and therefore lonely. It is in the dying, as the Bible passage tells us, that we harvest the fruit.

When Unamuno tells us to leave what's dead in ourselves, I think he is advising us not to spread about our despair or our self-pity—those things that won't give any harvest—but only to share what is alive in us. In sharing our gifts and talents with the world, we give ourselves away—we die a little—and in that way, we reap the harvest:

> *from your work you will be able one day to*
> *gather yourself.*

Finally, I can think of no better footnote to Unamuno's

stirring poem than these lines by W. H. Murray, leader of the
Scottish Himalaya Expedition:

> Until one is committed, there is hesitancy, the chance
> to draw back. Concerning all acts of initiative (and
> creation), there is one elementary truth the igno-
> rance of which kills countless ideas and splendid
> plans: that the moment one definitely commits
> oneself, then Providence moves too. All sorts of
> things occur to help one that would never other-
> wise have occurred. A whole stream of events issues
> from the decision, raising in one's favour all man-
> ner of unforeseen incidents and meetings and
> material assistance, which no man could have
> dreamed would have come his way.
>
> Whatever you do, or dream you can do, begin it.
> Boldness has genius, power, and magic in it. Begin
> it now.[4]

4

UNFOLD YOUR OWN MYTH

by Rumi *(Excerpt)*

Who gets up early to discover the moment light begins?
. . . .

Who lets a bucket down and brings
up a flowing prophet? Or like Moses goes for fire
and finds what burns inside the sunrise?

Jesus slips into a house to escape enemies,
And opens a door to the other world.
Solomon cuts open a fish, and there's a gold ring.
Omar storms in to kill the prophet
and leaves with blessings.
. . . .

But don't be satisfied with stories, how things
have gone with others. Unfold
your own myth, without complicated explanation,

so everyone will understand the passage,
We have opened you.

Start walking toward Shams. Your legs will get heavy
and tired. Then comes the moment
of feeling the wings you've grown,
lifting.

Don't Be Satisfied with Stories

[D] *on't be satisfied with stories,* Rumi exclaims just a few lines into this poem. Never mind the pouring images of getting up early to discover the way light returns, of flowing prophets, of slitting fish and finding a gold coin; storming in to kill the prophet Mohammed and leaving—who would ever have believed it?—with blessings. Not to mention slipping into a house to escape enemies and opening a door to the other world. Never mind all that. These are beautiful stories, yes; but they are not yours.

Stories are a double-edged sword. They can fire your imagination to act on its own lights, or they can so preoccupy your mind with the dramas of other people that you never get to live your own. This is one reason why people become seminar junkies, trailing from one charismatic speaker to the next. It is easier to listen to others, or to read about their exciting lives, than it is to live fully one's own. Gossip columns, too, thrive on our propensity to live vicariously in the shadow of someone else's (apparently) brighter light.

The lives of the saints can do the same thing. More than once, I have spent an evening with Rumi's poetry during which I have found myself stewing in a vague, mystical soup of feelings that actually had me believing in the moment that I was living through what Rumi was speaking of. It was a kind of auto-eroticism with poetry, a substitute for the real experience. Whereas, in reality, I hadn't even begun to know the heat of the fire in that man's chest.

In my twenties, I used to do something similar with the stories of the maverick spiritual teacher G. I. Gurdjieff, who describes a world of magicians, miracles, sages, remote monasteries in the mountains of Afghanistan, arduous treks across the Gobi desert, strange encounters at the pyramids of Giza, and much more, in his classic book, *Meetings with Remarkable Men*.[1] It was no contest: The glamour of Gurdjieff's tales far outshone my humdrum reality of earning a living in the gray light of London. I would daydream endlessly about exotic adventures, while living out my days with a generalized feeling of dissatisfaction and ennui. Waiting for the tube on a windswept and grubby platform deep down in the clay of London, I would chew with relish on a tale like the one Gurdjieff tells of financing his adventures by painting sparrows yellow and selling them as canaries in cages in the local market, somewhere in Azerbaijan.

Yet stories are indeed a double-edged sword, and we also need them. They can be a catalyst to action, to the lighting of the fire in our own life. I needed Gurdjieff's tales in my twenties. They fed a hunger in me—for meaning, for the big breath of the world—that my daily surroundings could never satisfy. And for all the daydreaming they spawned in me, they did in fact prompt me to follow my own story and set out on my own adventures. They inspired me to go to the Sahara desert and spend time out in the wasteland on my own; they also inspired me to go to Mount Athos, the finger of land that juts out into the Aegean, in northern Greece, where twenty-one Greek Orthodox monasteries have survived for the last thousand years, and where no woman has set foot in all that time.

Stories are what make us, many people once believed, not the other way around. This is why ancient cultures lived within the world of their stories, their myths. Their myths were living in the sense that they imbued with meaning the culture and the daily life of the individuals within it; they gave a potency to the most ordinary of acts—to hunting, to eating, to making love, to planting corn. Everything then was replete with meaning, by virtue of the stories that held the society together.

Today, we can still find our deepest longings and desires reflected in the stories to be found in great poetry and literature. A great poem, like this one, can point to the emerging pattern of your own life. You never know. One clue is the hair on the back of your neck, the way it can stand up at the end of a sentence. Or the sudden chill or heat that can flush through your body as some words leap off a page, seize you by the throat or open a gate in your heart. Gurdjieff's stories struck me that way; they became the catalyst that moved me to act out my own dreams.

Stories feed the imagination, which is our connection between who we are and who we may be, between our individual existence and the bigger stories of the race and the culture to which we belong. And yes, the imagination is also the connection between our own tiny ship of a soul and the vastness of the ocean on which it sails. We have always needed stories to stoke the imagination's fires, and doubtless we always shall—despite the postmodern cry that realism, characters, and their stories, are dead.

In an essay for *The New Yorker,* Jonathan Franzen wrote that, for the postmodern writer, characters are "feeble, suspect constructs, like the author himself, like the human soul. Nevertheless, to my shame, I seemed to need them."

Franzen isn't alone: We all need stories. It is because they can be a source of inspiration, the match to start our own fire, that I am presenting these poems and writing this book. As long as we remember to use them that way, and not as a substitute for the living of our own true life. Which is why Rumi exhorts us in the way he does, to

> *Unfold*
> *your own myth, without complicated explanation,*

Unfold, he says, not *make it,* or *make it up.* Intentionally allow what is already there to come into the light of day. It's an attitude he is speaking about, I think, rather than any willful doing. Laurens van der Post casts a further light on unfolding your own myth with these words:

> I think everything has a story, and by following our own individual stories and the stories which face the central issues of one's life and one's time, if one follows that, one changes things. The story will do it.[2]

It's all in the following of what's already there—of who's already there. And what is there, wanting to unfold, van der Post says, is our own authentic story, the reason we were born in the first place. And when Rumi tells us not to be satisfied with stories, he doesn't just mean the stories other people tell us; he's also talking about the stories we tell ourselves. The ones that keep us treading water for thirty years without even noticing it until suddenly we have a bypass and it all starts to seem too late. The stories in our head about what our parents thought we should be, about how inadequate we are, our lack of talent, or about how we were always destined for great things, if only someone could recognize us for who we really are.

Don't be satisfied with these stories, he says. And don't be fooled by success stories either: by the wonderful business you have built or the books you have written. These can be a prison as much as anything else. They can seduce you with a freeze frame—a solid picture of who you think you are—and keep you running on the same wheel for the rest of your life without hearing even a whisper of a deeper sound, a sound inside you that has been singing since the day you were born. Colorful adventures can do the same thing, like the time you went to the desert or to some rocky Greek outpost all on your own. They have their place, stories like these, as long as we don't feed off them for years afterward instead of continuing to follow the deeper story that has no name.

No, our authentic story does not originate in the brain and its complexes. Who is to say where it comes from? From our genetic material, perhaps, or from the "soul's code," as the psychologist James Hillman put it.[3] It doesn't matter where it comes from, says Rumi. It doesn't matter where a tree comes from, or the wind. You don't need *complicated explanations.* All you need in the first instance is a willingness to acknowledge that there is only one of you on this earth, and the simplicity and the courage to claim that uniqueness, however it may express itself.

When just one person lives their own true story, the ripples will fan outward and touch everyone. We are never separate from our essential, individual pattern, or myth, so we can never fully objectify it and talk about it. It is the essence of who we are. We can only live the truth of it in the present moment, even if we tell stories about it later to convey the experience. That is also why no *complicated explanation* is necessary. You just act. That is all. And this is the clue about the kind of action that stems from direct knowing: It exudes a profound simplicity, and also certainty. Others cannot help but catch the scent of that kind of action. Despite themselves, they will intuitively, below the thresholds of the words, grasp the meaning of the passage *We have opened you.*

This opening just happens, for no reason, anywhere—on a rainy day in a room with creaky floorboards and a wall lined with books; on a windy hill one summer's afternoon, or in bed just as the eyes are beginning to feel the glimmer of light through the window. It happens in dreams. It happens especially in dreams, because the conscious mind and all of its stories have been put on hold and subterranean currents can rise to the surface.

It happened to a man I know in India, a simple farmer, in an unusually dramatic way. He dreamed one night that a man came to him and kissed him on the cheek. On waking, the farmer felt profoundly at peace. Some weeks later, he saw a photograph of the man in his dream in a newspaper. He was a great saint who had died some years previously. The farmer had never heard of him, but his life had already been changed by the saint's presence. Within days of his dream, people began to come to him for spiritual advice. The farmer had no spiritual training or discipline, and little education. Yet he found himself responding to their concerns as well as he could. More dreams followed, and now, unassuming as ever, that farmer—his name is Nanagaru—is a solace and inspiration to people all over southern India.[4] *We have opened you.*

Start walking toward Shams.

Shams was Rumi's teacher, the one who, with his fierce and loving gaze, lifted the veils from Rumi's heart. That gaze reduced to ashes all of Rumi's scholarship, his knowledge of the Koran, his reputation, everything, and left his inner-most core revealed. The word *Shams* means, literally, the sun. When, by grace, the veils, like the mist at dawn, are burned away from our heart, others see the opening and are changed in some way. Very few of us will ever meet someone like Shams in the flesh, but the sun he represents also lives in our core, and I believe that to stand in its light is to take on our own unique story, whatever that may be.

No one, least of all Rumi, ever said it was simply a matter of making the decision. If only it were so easy! No, that is only the beginning. Rumi assures us that our legs *will get heavy and tired.* Sometimes—often, even—we will feel like quitting. It will seem so much more reasonable to take a respectable job, rather than to follow your passion; to do what others expect of you, to compromise and at least, if nothing else, to fulfill your obligations. The dream in you, your own true dharma, as the Buddhists call it, is a tender thing, easily crushed by the demands of the world. Remember David Whyte's lines,

> *I want to know*
> *if you are prepared to live in the world*
> *with its harsh need to change you.*[5]

If you persist in walking the one path that is yours, says Rumi, despite all the resistance you are bound to encounter, then you will feel something different.

> *Then comes the moment*
> *of feeling the wings you've grown,*
> *lifting.*

You will feel that levity, that freedom in the human heart, which, however challenging your circumstances may be, can give wings to the life you are living.

5

HAVE YOU EVER TRIED TO ENTER THE LONG BLACK BRANCHES?

by Mary Oliver

Have you ever tried to enter the long black branches
  of other lives—
tried to imagine what the crisp fringes, full of honey,
  hanging
from the branches of the young locust trees, in early summer,
  feel like?

Do you think this world is only an entertainment for you?

Never to enter the sea and notice how the water divides
  with perfect courtesy, to let you in!
Never to lie down with the grass, as though you were the grass!
Never to leap to the air as you open your wings over
  the dark acorn of your heart!

No wonder we hear, in your mournful voice, the complaint
  that something is missing from your life!

Who can open the door who does not reach for the latch?

Who can travel the miles who does not put one foot
    in front of the other, all attentive to what presents itself
    continually?
Who will behold the inner chamber who has not observed
    with admiration, even with rapture, the outer stone?

Well, there is time left—
fields everywhere invite you into them.

And who will care, who will chide you if you wander away
    from wherever you are, to look for your soul?

Quickly, then, get up, put on your coat, leave your desk!

To put one's foot into the door of the grass, which is
    the mystery, which is death as well as life, and
    not be afraid!

To set one's foot in the door of death, and be overcome
    with amazement!

To sit down in front of the weeds, and imagine
    god the ten-fingered, sailing out of his house of straw,

nodding this way and that way, to the flowers of the
    present hour,

to the song falling out of the mockingbird's pink mouth,

to the tiplets of the honeysuckle, that have opened
  in the night.

To sit down, like a weed among weeds, and rustle in the wind!

~

Listen, are you breathing just a little, and calling it a life?

While the soul, after all, is only a window,
and the opening of the window no more difficult
than the wakening from a little sleep.

~

Only last week I went out among the thorns and said
  to the wild roses:
deny me not,
but suffer my devotion.
Then, all afternoon, I sat among them. Maybe

I even heard a curl or two of music, damp and rouge-red,
hurrying from their stubby buds, from their delicate watery bodies.

~

For how long will you continue to listen to those dark shouters,
  caution and prudence?

Fall in! Fall in!

~

A woman standing in the weeds.
A small boat flounders in the deep waves, and what's coming next
    is coming with its own heave and grace.

~

Meanwhile, once in a while, I have chanced, among the quick things,
    upon the immutable.
What more could one ask?

And I would touch the faces of the daisies,
and I would bow down
to think about it.

That was then, which hasn't ended yet.

Now the sun begins to swing down. Under the peach-light,
I cross the fields and the dunes, I follow the ocean's edge.

I climb. I backtrack.
I float.
I ramble my way home.

Fall In! Fall In!

Mary Oliver's body of work is a pure litany of rapture, a song of ecstatic praise in honor of the physical world. She seems to spend her days out in the fields and along the ocean shore marveling at whelks and geese, rabbits, roses, hermit crabs, gannets, poppies, the sunrise, and moths. I, on the other hand, have become more of a city person as I have grown older. I follow her vicariously, more often than not, to the fields and the seashore, by way of her poems. In reading a poem of hers, like this one, I can feel the fire of life rekindled, my place in the natural world restored.

To tell the truth, these days I am a city person who spends much of his time in a cabin in the woods. Here I am now, sitting in my cabin in upstate New York, looking out of the window onto the long gray branches of the birch trees swaying in the dappled light of a late afternoon. I look down again to the first few lines of Mary Oliver's poem, and I acknowledge to myself that I have not entered those branches today, nor yesterday. Cabin or no cabin, I am, in this moment, and more often than not, at home in my intellect, and the trees remain beyond the window.

In this sense, her poem itself becomes a field for me, one of those "other lives" that I can enter to feel the pulse of the living world again. On the one hand, she is referring to the fields where the lilies and the corn grow, real fields with weeds and mud and running things; but I don't often go there. That is why, for someone like me, her poem itself becomes a field—and I think she intends this. One of the differences between poetry and prose is that a good poem invites an immersion into direct experience. An attentive reading, especially a reading aloud, is an absorption, not just into the subject matter and the meaning, but into the body of the poem, the lilt, the sway, the texture of it. You breathe it in, and you sway along. That is why a good poem is its own message, its own magic. Prose, on the other hand, more often than not tells you *about* things; you receive the experience at one remove. But Oliver's poem is a life form, a field, one you can lie down in, *as though you were the grass!*

And when she says, almost halfway through this poem, that

fields everywhere invite you into them

she is suggesting that not only a poem, but anything, any present moment of our lives, can become a field where we can experience life directly. Poetry, art, music, all these are fields we can enter. Being in love is a full immersion, and the love of our life, if we have one, holds our own heart in its hand for us to see, if we would only look. The beauty of certain cities, a face on the subway, a shaft of light in a filthy street, a plastic bag dancing in the wind (remember the film,

American Beauty?): Anything can open the door to the won-drous heart if we are willing and ready for it to be so. Such moments can fall upon us anywhere, at any time, and espe-cially if we allow ourselves to be prone to them. That is how, and why, those fields of Oliver's can be truly everywhere.

How does she invite us into this, the field of her poem? The meaning, the sense of it, is striking enough, but if the literal meaning of the words were all she wanted to convey, she could have written a paragraph. It is the literal body of the poem, the breath of it, which truly gathers us up in its rhythms, its sounds, its cadences and sentence structures, and holds us in its spell.

If you read the first half of the poem out loud, you will feel the urgency in it, almost breathless, all repeating excla-mations, commands, and questions, culminating in the line *Listen, are you breathing. . . .* Then, like a piece of music shift-ing from fanfare to adagio, everything changes to a slower, softer pace, to a mood of musing and devotion. As the breath of the poem and the shapes of its words enter you, you become the poem, and the poem becomes you. In the same way that the wind over the weeds enters you, or the song of the insects in the wildflowers enters you.

There is also the shock of a line like this, the kind of line that flies off the page and blows my embers to flame:

Do you think this world is only an entertainment for you?

Now she really has my attention. Mary Oliver is far from being just another nature poet. She is not content with merely drawing us into some beautiful contemplation of the natural world. No, she wants us to wake up to how we tend to live so easily on the edge of life. Are we going to fritter away our days without even noticing them pass by? Can we afford any half-heartedness in the time remaining to us?

I wonder how her line strikes you. Is the way you respond to nature the same as the way you inhabit your life in general? Seeing it all, as I do through my cabin window, with a certain critical perspective? Is this the way you read a poem? Never entering any reality beyond your own? (*Leave your desk!*, she cries, later in the poem—leave the place where you make your living, pay the bills, answer the phone.) To look at nature through a window is to see it as a passing show, she reminds me, a pretty entertainment for our eyes that we can watch at a safe distance. Are we always going to live life from a safe distance? Oliver is asking. Never to get our toes wet in the ocean, never to lie down in the grass, with the grass, *as though you were grass!*

Oliver's words are working their way through my skin. Excuse me for an afternoon while I take a walk in real pastures, neglected too long. The fire in that line, the one about the world being an entertainment, is smoking me out of my hut and into the woods. It is the fire that burns through much of Oliver's work. She wants us to take responsibility for being in this life; to engage with the world of living, breathing, walking, creeping, fluttering things, instead of wandering through life in a daze, like bystanders at a sideshow. And of all poets, Oliver is not one to be coy about making bold declarations, straight from the hip—like the line about the world being an entertainment. That's why I love her work: Not only is it resonant with beauty, it also delivers a slap to my dreaming head just when I need it.

And then,

> *Never to leap to the air as you open your wings over*
> *the dark acorn of your heart!*

Is she talking to *me*? A mighty oak tree buried as seed in *my* heart's core? Something waiting to soar into life and fill the air with its long branches and the song of bright birds whose names I do not as yet even know? Well, and why not? Why not, then, leap into the air at the thought?

Because, as she says, my feet are too often bound by the complaint that something is missing from my life. Because my eyes are too often either looking backward or forward, but oh, so rarely at what is right in front of me, here and now. Oh, the sweet, seductive longing for who knows what, as long as it isn't what I already have! Oliver definitely has my number. "The gap," between what is and what could be, or might have been, has for too long been an intrinsic part of my experience.

Occasionally, I walk into The Gap and fill the vacuum with a new piece of clothing. Somewhat more often, I have filled it with a French pastry, one of those butter-cream seductions you can find in Payard Patisserie on Lexington Avenue. The gap will disappear for a whole afternoon after one of those. Then, I can fill the emptiness with a glance at the long pair of legs whose owner has just passed me on the street. But most of all, I tend to fill it with a vague nostalgia for somewhere else, like the south of France, Avignon, for example; or one of those villages in Tuscany, San Quirico d'Orcia, say, whose name, all on its own, is enough to make you certain that life over there must have a radiance and meaning that could never be found on West 22nd Street, much less here, in a cabin with a window onto long black branches.

Then there is the spiritual yearning, the longing for something that can never be found in the visible world. Call it the eternal, the supernal, the sempiternal; there's a good enough word, it doesn't matter what we call it, since all words fall short. As long as I am bound up with a fixation on the heavens above, on gâteaux, and on San Quirico, I am never going to have much energy left over for the branches of young locust trees in early summer, or whatever else the day happens to bring before me. Heaven, Mary Oliver reminds us in all of her poems, is nowhere if not here, right where we are. That, I think, is her meaning in this poem. Or so, in any event, I take it to be. Whatever pulls us away from the radiant present to somewhere or something else is the very thing that can drain our life away.

Who can open the door who does not reach for the latch?

We reach for the latch when we slip out from under our own self-absorption and, in a moment of self-forgetfulness, willingly step out into the big living world that was there all along—the world of long black branches, of other people, of honking geese and city sounds and whelks and crashing waves. The self we forget is the one absorbed in its own thoughts and fantasies. It is someone else in us, an ever-present, wide-awake one, who knows to participate in the world by actively engaging with it. By showing up.

If we remain lost in our hopes and fears, our longings and dreamings, we will not even notice the sun breaking through the banks of clouds. Look up and out; this is always Oliver's byword—or even down, at the stone at your foot. Look with your whole heart, and that undivided attention to the physical universe, out beyond all self-preoccupation, may be enough to strike the match that catches your heart on fire.

Perhaps you have not made that leap (of no distance at all).

> *Well, there is time left—*
> *fields everywhere invite you into them.*

> *And who will care, who will chide you if you wander away*
> *from wherever you are, to look for your soul?*

Where we are is usually in a swell of duties and plans and wonderings and schemings. No one will notice if we drop out of those for a while to look up at where we really are. And Oliver is right, as I remembered again only this afternoon: It can make a huge difference to go further, to fling on your coat and change the scenery for a while. To go for a walk. For the first time in weeks I heard the crunch of stiff grasses beneath my feet, felt the nodding weight of a branch laden with ice, sensed the squirrel's eager teeth on a nut. How many poems, inspirations, realizations, breakthroughs, have come upon human beings when they were out walking the dog? Or just plain strolling?

Though Mary Oliver is counseling a particular kind of walk, one with close attention to details, the details of what lies around us—the grass, the weeds, the song falling from the mockingbird's pink mouth. If we enter the world with everything that we are, we shall find there, she says, not only the mirror of our own life, but also of our death:

> *To put one's foot into the door of the grass, which is*
> *the mystery, which is death as well as life, and*
> *not be afraid!*

> *To set one's foot in the door of death, and be overcome*
> *with amazement!*

To enter the world completely is to step out of our skin and encounter the mystery, which is always death as well as life: the death of the ever-watchful observer in us, and the death of the known in the face of the inherently unknowable. Can we enter the mystery in amazement rather than in fear? That is Oliver's wish for herself, and she is urging the same quality of amazement on us. Again, not an amazement that makes of us a safe observer (look at those beautiful weeds!), but one that joins us to the weeds themselves in their rustling; one in which we become weed, and the rustling.

And then, another of Mary Oliver's wonderful "Wake up and live" lines:

Listen, are you breathing just a little, and calling it a life?

I would take the whole poem just for that one line. It reminds me of a verse, written two thousand years ago, by the author of Revelations:

> I know thy works, that thou art neither cold nor hot:
> I would thou wert cold or hot. So then because thou
> art lukewarm, and neither cold nor hot, I will spew
> thee out of my mouth.[1]

Oliver's line is that strong to my ears. I once heard Billy Collins say that poets are of the species *homo linearis*, Line Man. The line is everything in a poem. Rhythm, sound, meaning, length, everything must be for a reason, and not a single syllable can be wasted or out of place. That is one thing that distinguishes it from prose. Mary Oliver is one of the preeminent line-makers. And this particular line is a string of words you are unlikely to forget. I mean, just notice your breathing now. Are you, in fact, breathing just a little? Of course. Most of us are. And she is on to us. It seems, with a few dynamic exceptions, to be part of the human predicament to live for much of the time on the air in only one lung. But then someone says something, and we notice, we draw a deep breath, and another life becomes possible to us in that instant.

After the "breathing" line, the lilt of the poem changes, the mood, more reflective. It really isn't so difficult, she suggests, with a sudden forbearance:

> *While the soul, after all, is only a window,*
> *and the opening of the window no more difficult*
> *than the wakening from a little sleep.*

We need to make some kind of gesture, an active movement, in order to let life in, although the movement is so subtle, so slight, no more than the raising of the eyelids after a nap. So what stops us from opening the window?

What stops us from opening the window is *listening* to the shouting voices of caution and prudence. The theme of listening, woven into the whole body of the poem, becomes crucial here, and it culminates with the line in which she demands we turn our listening toward her: *Listen, are you breathing. . . .*

Caution and prudence have their place in life, but we so often heed their calls when we least need them. If we follow their every command, we shall forever be teetering on the edge of life, of wholehearted experience, keeping a safe distance with the use of our dividing intellect and powers of analysis, but also with our cynicism and doubt, staying—or so, at least, we would like to think—in control of our experience and environment. These few lines, which Oliver has put in italics, are all the more urgent coming, as they do, in the middle of a developing lyrical calm. Don't think, she cries, don't listen to these voices,

Fall in! Fall in!

Oliver's image of the sea journey,

> *A small boat flounders in deep waves, and what's coming next*
> *is coming with its own heave and grace.*

makes me think of the tiny boat of the soul, and how what is coming to it is coming with *its own heave*—for it is momentous, what emerges from slumber when the soul awakens—even if it comes on the fine air of grace. The new life, in which we are no longer merely lukewarm, as Revelations puts it, is too big for our minds to understand. So why, then, should we worry?

This degree of attentive surrender to the beauty of the natural world is nothing less than a religious, or rather spiritual activity. For Oliver, I suspect, it is her devotional practice, a discipline as committed as any monk's in his cell. [*S*]*uffer my devotion*, she pleads with the roses, as she prepares to sit down with them all afternoon and listen for their music.

> *And I would touch the faces of the daisies,*
> *and I would bow down*
> *to think about it.*

The scientist who studies apes or dandelions for a lifetime must know a similar devotion. Mary Oliver offers us hers through her poem. And her last three lines, as simple as they sound, carry an echo to my ears of an opening door, the door that leads us back to where we started from; to the place beyond the setting sun at the end of her poem:

> *I climb. I backtrack.*
> *I float.*
> *I ramble my way home.*

As if to say that the primordial innocence (reflected in the utter simplicity of these lines) that prevails when we slip the noose of self-preoccupation and join the living world is the signature of our original face. The one we had before we were born and will continue to have even when death has taken everything else away.

6

THE LAYERS

by Stanley Kunitz

I have walked through many lives,
some of them my own,
and I am not who I was,
though some principle of being
abides, from which I struggle
not to stray.
When I look behind,
as I am compelled to look
before I can gather strength
to proceed on my journey,
I see the milestones dwindling
toward the horizon
and the slow fires trailing
from the abandoned camp-sites,
over which scavenger angels
wheel on heavy wings.
Oh, I have made myself a tribe
out of my true affections,
and my tribe is scattered!

How shall the heart be reconciled
to its feast of losses?
In a rising wind
the manic dust of my friends,
those who fell along the way,
bitterly stings my face.
Yet I turn, I turn,
exulting somewhat,
with my will intact to go
wherever I need to go,
and every stone on the road
precious to me.
In my darkest night,
when the moon was covered
and I roamed through wreckage,
a nimbus-clouded voice
directed me:
"Live in the layers,
not on the litter."
Though I lack the art
to decipher it,
no doubt the next chapter
in my book of transformations
is already written.
I am not done with my changes.

I Am Not Who I Was

Stanley Kunitz was in his seventies when he wrote this poem. Today, at ninety-eight, he is still writing, the oldest active poet alive. Still now, at his venerable age, he does not consider himself "done with my changes." One of the great American poets of the twentieth century, and twice poet laureate, he is a man dedicated to the aesthetic life, to the persistent aspiration toward truth and beauty. His daily existence is dedicated to the life of the soul; and the soul of a man like Kunitz never stops flowering.

He has passed through many lives, not just those of others, but many that he himself took on and then later let fall away. Or perhaps some of them were torn from him by the winds of fate, by circumstance, or by others. I know that his first wife, whom he loved greatly, suddenly disappeared from his life one day, and that he never heard from her again. Then, within a short span of time, and not long before writing "The Layers," he suffered the loss of his mother and two sisters, as well as several of his dearest friends, including the poet Theodore Roethke and the artist Philip Guston. With great dignity, he speaks in this poem of the losses he has known and what it is that survives when all else is gone.

However solid and secure our own lives may seem, the people and circumstances of the present moment will not always be here. This is what Kunitz came painfully to understand at the time of writing this poem, and it is true now for you and me. Like him, we might do well to ponder those lives we have touched and passed through, and also those personal incarnations we have lived through and then exchanged for the next one, like so many overcoats. Or perhaps, at times, the experience has been more like that of a bud nipped by an early frost. Taken too soon, it seems. There are many ways in which we step out of one life into another.

I wonder sometimes about the traces I have left in those lives that are no longer a part of my own—not visibly a part, that is, since I believe that nothing and no one ever really leaves without some trace that flickers on in the synapses. Whatever happened to my favorite schoolmaster? My first lover? My first wife, from whom I parted almost twenty years ago? Where does it go, the tremor you yourself may have felt, the first time you touched the cheek of the man who was to be your husband; whose bed you shared for so many years, and who is now in another life?

Everything passes. Is it sad? Is it a relief? Sometimes one, sometimes the other, but it is what it is, always, and the spectrum of feelings it generates also passes in its turn. Is there anything, then, that abides?

There is, Kunitz assures us, "some principle of being" from which he struggles not to stray. I find that a beautiful thing, the acknowledgment of something in him that remains, a titanium vein, indestructible essence, that survives all vicissitudes. If only we could let our sense of identity rest in that, rather than be swept up in all the passing moods and conditions of our life, our experience of what happens to us would be different indeed. But that is just the point: We *don't* know that rest; at least, not most of the time. Most of the time, we are wholly absorbed in the passing show. And yet, I think that's okay. It's completely okay to be human, to be broken open in our frailties and sorrows, lifted up in our joys and elations, and to know that we are not in control of our lives.

Because that is the realization that makes us bow down. It is the awareness of his weakness, his frailty, which prompts Kunitz to struggle not to stray from this principle of being that he knows exists at his core. Even though he is approaching his first century, he still must struggle, because he will be human to the end. It is never easy being true to the Person we are. There is no resting place. As soon as we are comfortable with what we once knew in our bones, we have lost it. The truth of our being can only be lived. The telling of it is too often a husk we indulge in to pass the time, to pump up our image, or to give color to that ungraspable passage, the feeling of our life.

What then, is this principle of being that Stanley Kunitz is speaking of? Some core he knows to be true, yes—but not, I think, a belief in this or that code, moral or otherwise. Perhaps it is something you can recognize in the photograph of yourself when you were two years old. The same look in your eyes that has survived a lifetime. I have a photograph of myself at that age, sitting erect in one of those big wheeled prams of the forties, wool coat buttoned up to my neck, blond curls (long gone), eyes gazing wide at the camera. The same feisty curiosity, there then, as it is now. That early look in your eyes is an indication of who you are, your unique individuality, nothing learned or acquired.

But there is more. This principle of being is not just a given at birth. The look in the two-year-old's eyes is the raw material out of which something is forged during a lifetime. And that something is the soul. One afternoon in his Greenwich apartment, which he shares with Elise, his third wife, Kunitz told me of a realization he once had. He was teaching poetry to a class, when he suddenly understood that the first great task of the poetic imagination is to create the self—the person who will write the poem. "In the writing," he said, "you are making yourself." I was reminded of Keats, who spoke of life as a "vale of soul-making." [1] And of Gerard Manley Hopkins, too, who spoke of the "taste of oneself" as being the most important thing we can know.[2]

Sometimes the voice of the soul directly challenges the structure of our personal life. It may require us to leave an empty marriage, for example. Or prompt us to move on when our work has ceased to engage us. Authenticity and daily life are not always an easy match. That is why Kunitz has gone through so many changes. No wonder, too, even at ninety-eight, Kunitz has to struggle not to stray from his own interior sense of truth. His struggle is an inspiration to all of us who enter his poem.

Stanley Kunitz has tended his famous garden in Provincetown for decades. He understands the value of layers of compost and what can grow from them. His garden is a living metaphor for his dedication to the work of "soul-making."

> *When I look behind,*
> *as I am compelled to look*
> *before I can gather strength*
> *to proceed on my journey, . . .*

We, too, can look to our own, individual history for support and strength to continue our journey. The past will support us in the degree that, like Kunitz, we bear witness to it—acknowledge its joys and sorrows, successes and failures, instead of denying it by looking away and only forward. Someone as old as Kunitz knows the weight and the value of history. He understands that loss, death, defeat are an intrinsic part of any human journey. Yet so, too, can the warmth of companionship be,

> *. . . the slow fires trailing*
> *from the abandoned camp-sites, . . .*

The love and friendship Kunitz has known in his life, even if the people in question are long gone, continue to feed not only the "scavenger" angels, but him, too. As I am also sustained by loves that have enriched and colored my own passage here, even if those loved ones are in my life no longer.

It is not possible fully to embrace the gift of love without also accepting the inevitability of loss. Kunitz has been generous enough of heart to make a whole tribe of his true affections, and the entire tribe is now scattered. Can we be that generous, that substantial in our love, that we are willing to hold nothing back, even though everything shall eventually be taken away?

> *How shall the heart be reconciled*
> *to its feast of losses?*

He cries out! How? There is no answer. No easy platitude or soothing advice will do. The poet Marie Howe once told Stanley Kunitz that the death of her brother John felt to her as if something had her in its mouth and was chewing her up.[3] "It is," Kunitz told her. "And you must wait to see who you'll be when it's done with you."

In the full embrace of his own loss something stirs in him:

> *Yet I turn, I turn, . . .*

The word *turn* is used to describe the place in a sonnet where there is "a change in direction of narrative," and this line is indeed the moment of the *turn* in the poem, as Kunitz moves on from the past,

> *exulting somewhat,*
> *with my will intact to go*
> *wherever I need to go,*
> *and every stone on the road*
> *precious to me.*

The kind of will he is speaking of is not the familiar self-will that pushes us to do what we feel we must even though we don't want to. No, he means the will that arises from the principle of being in him that abides through all successes and failures, all loves and losses. It is the essence of who he is, and it will take him where he needs to go. He has that much faith in it. So much so, that he knows that even the stones along the way are precious, that they have their part in his journey.

No accident, then, that the moment of revelation comes in his darkest hour, when all seems lost and he is wandering alone in what seems to be the wreckage of his life:

> *"Live in the layers,*
> *not on the litter."*

Stanley Kunitz himself still cannot fully decipher these lines. How can you explain revelation? They came to him one night at the end of a terrifying dream, a voice from out of a cloud speaking a riddle as strange as any from the Delphic oracle of ancient Greece. He woke immediately and wrote down the lines. Soon afterward, the whole poem flowed from these two lines.

Revelation is by nature inscrutable. You can wonder, you can let these lines work on you, you can sense their drift, let them work their way into your blood, but you, like Stanley himself, will never reach the end of them. For me, to *live in the layers* implies responding to life from one's own depths, rather than being distracted by the flotsam and jetsam—the litter—of what happens on the surface. Kunitz told me that for him, the layers suggested all the changes we go through in a life, all the different roles and lives we have lived. To live in them is to claim them for our own; to affirm them and the way each of them has contributed to the making of our soul, that principle of being in us. In the French translation of this poem, the litter refers to the stretcher that bears the dead or the infirm. Whatever the meaning, what matters for Stanley Kunitz is that he realizes something astounding:

> *no doubt the next chapter*
> *in my book of transformations*
> *is already written.*

He realizes, first of all, that even at his age, his life is not over; that there is a next chapter. He sees, too, that each of the many lives he has walked through has played a part in the forging of his soul; that everything had its place, and that there is a sense and intelligence to his life journey that was there from the beginning. So much so, that his life feels like a book that is already written. And finally, after all the campfires he has left behind, after all the lives he has lived and shared, after all the years he has spent on this earth,

> *I am not done with my changes.*

The alchemical work of transformation—the turning of loss into a kind of gold, the opening to love despite all the pain—will continue for as long as he lives. This is surely the alchemical work, the real struggle we are here on earth for. The one that fortifies that principle of being that does not tarnish or rust. If there is anything that abides even after death, it is probably that.

7

SO MUCH HAPPINESS

by Naomi Shihab Nye

It is difficult to know what to do with so much happiness.
With sadness there is something to rub against,
a wound to tend with lotion and cloth.
When the world falls in around you, you have pieces to
  pick up,
something to hold in your hands, like ticket stubs
  or change.

But happiness floats.
It doesn't need you to hold it down.
It doesn't need anything.
Happiness lands on the roof of the next house, singing,
and disappears when it wants to.
You are happy either way.
Even the fact that you once lived in a peaceful tree house
and now live over a quarry of noise and dust
cannot make you unhappy.
Everything has a life of its own,

it too could wake up filled with possibilities
of coffee cake and ripe peaches,
and love even the floor which needs to be swept,
the soiled linens and scratched records. . . .

Since there is no place large enough
to contain so much happiness,
you shrug, you raise your hands, and it flows out of you
into everything you touch. You are not responsible.
You take no credit, as the night sky takes no credit
for the moon, but continues to hold it, and share it,
and in that way, be known.

Happiness Needs No Reason

At first glance the happiness filling this poem might seem so exalted that your own seems to pale in comparison. I would respond that Naomi Shihab Nye is describing something so simple and accessible that we might not even notice it when it alights on our shoulder. I am reminded of the letter John Keats wrote to John Taylor on February 27, 1818, in which he says:

> Poetry should strike the reader as a wording of his own highest thoughts, and appear almost as a Remembrance.[1]

I believe that this degree of happiness is intrinsic to who we are, and that the work of this poem is to remind us of that.

Nye hits the mark, though, when she says that we find it easier to remember and speak about our aches and pains, our sorrows and sadness.

> *With sadness there is something to rub against, . . .*

Isn't that the truth! Sadness has a gravity that can weigh down both body and mind to such a degree that to think of anything else—even to think of looking up—can become almost inconceivable. Sadness can turn to self-pity and become a lid to seal away our happiness for years. Depression can become addictive, a whole way of life. Notice how many verbs there are in these few lines, and all of them referring to *doing* something in response to sadness: *to rub against . . . to tend . . . pieces to pick up . . . to hold. . . .* As if difficulty and sadness require action; as if they generate the need to feel in control. This need to fix things, to have some practical response, is precisely what our Western culture considers natural.

Happiness, on the other hand, just happens, and in its own time and place. It comes and goes as it pleases, and all your personal will can do in response, Nye tells us later in the poem, is simply to *shrug, . . . raise your hands, . . . take no credit. . . .* Happiness is far less tangible than sadness, more difficult to put your finger on, even to give a name to. It *floats.* We can have no control over it, and in this sense, happiness goes against the grain in Western culture. The kind of happiness that Naomi Shihab Nye is speaking of, that is.

> *It is difficult to know what to do with so much happiness.*

From the very first line, you can be sure that we are not talking the kind of happiness that comes from a full shopping cart. Not that Thomas Jefferson's notion of the "pursuit of happiness," as inscribed in the Bill of Rights for the benefit of all Americans, was ever meant to infer the right of all to an endless supply of consumer goods. Yet—yet, somehow, his credo was usurped somewhere down the centuries to mean just that.

No wonder, then, that many people today are wary of even using the word *happy* to describe themselves, as if such a condition were shorthand for a life of bland contentment resulting from material well-being and also, perhaps, from a stable and secure family life. "The useful monotony of happiness," Carol Shields calls this in her novel *Unless*.[2] Wealth and familial stability are conditions to be profoundly grateful for, but as all too many know, they do not come with a guarantee of happiness.

Having all of our everyday ducks in a row—a satisfying job, a good relationship, a good income—is, for most of us, a rare enough experience that, when it happens, we could be forgiven for feeling that we have everything we could ever hope for.

But as good as everyday contentment can be—and let there be no mistake, it is something many people would die for—it can turn on a dime as long as it is dependent on outer conditions. It is hardly what Jefferson meant by happiness. The Founding Father was a child of the Enlightenment. He believed ardently in the power of the individual human soul to govern itself. Self-government meant for him the development of a mind independent of external influences, the formation of an authentic self. Keats's term for this process was *soul-making*. Happiness, Jefferson believed, was the fruit of this inner development.

Nye's poem echoes these aspirations of Jefferson in important ways, but it also takes the experience of happiness in a lighter, more ecstatic direction than perhaps the gravitas of the Founding Father could allow him.

> *It doesn't need you to hold it down.*
> *It doesn't need anything.*

Happiness cannot be pinned down, even by the name of happiness, even by a poem, though this poem certainly gives us the taste of it. You can't put your finger on it. It doesn't need any one set of circumstances in order to appear. It just appears, for no reason,

> *and disappears when it wants to.*
> *You are happy either way.*
> *Even the fact that you once lived in a peaceful tree house*
> *and now live over a quarry of noise and dust*
> *cannot make you unhappy.*

Nye, like Jefferson, is saying here that essential happiness cannot be disturbed by outer conditions. Whether you live in beautiful surroundings or on the edge of a working quarry makes no difference to happiness because its source, finally, is not in the world of contingencies. Happiness is an expression of our intrinsic nature, which has no reason for anything other than the fact of its existence. I think of those geysers in New Zealand, the water spouting warm straight out of the dark earth.

I have known something of this happiness on trains. There is a sense of freedom that can happen in travel which for me is happiness itself—a freedom from the weight of my preoccupations; from the thickness of my own habitual sense of self, and the stories I weave about my life. In his wonderfully quirky book *The Art of Travel*, Alain de Botton says this:

> It is not necessarily at home that we best encounter our true selves. The furniture insists that we cannot change because it does not; the domestic setting keeps us tethered to the person we are in ordinary life, who may not be who we essentially are.[3]

I remember being on a train heading for the South of France, where, as a student of French at university, I was to spend six months at the Université de Toulouse. On that long, slow ride south from the gray of northern Europe, I was suspended between one world and the next. I had nothing to do, because the train was doing it for me—carrying me where I needed to go. My mind, freed from any necessity, lulled by the old-fashioned clickety-clack of the train, and by the lazy drone of the station master as we pulled into a station ("Limoges!" "Brive-la Gaillarde!" "Cahors!") fell into what I can only describe as a quiet elation. I was alone in my carriage, with no thought of the future that awaited me, nor any lingering reminiscence of the world I had left behind in England. There was only the present, the fields and the villages passing by, and the smell of the faded upholstery in the *train du Midi*. There was only I, myself, a condition in which, with Walt Whitman, I could say,

I believe in you, my soul . . .[4]

When I asked Vanda, an English friend of mine who now lives in California, to describe a moment of happiness she had known, she gave an answer that added another layer to my own experience. Before leaving England, she said, she had had a dream in which she saw a beach and a house where she felt she belonged. After moving to California a few months later, she was walking along Stinson Beach when suddenly, she saw before her the wooden house that had appeared in her dream. It was very distinctive, in a Japanese style, with huge windows and weeping birches planted at its corners. What filled her with happiness in that instant was not the fact that her dream had become manifest, so much as the sensation that her life had an underground intelligence to it. She felt held by life in that moment, safe in the feeling that her life was being led from a deeper source than her everyday hopes and fears. Everything is in hand; knowing that, it seems natural that you would

> *love even the floor which needs to be swept,*
> *the soiled linens and scratched records. . . .*

I wonder what the images in the last stanza of Naomi Shihab Nye's poem evoke for you. So much happiness, that it pours out of every gesture into everything you touch. And this:

> *. . . You are not responsible.*

We do not create this degree of happiness, remember, any more than we can create who we already are. It cannot be attained by a five-point plan or the latest self-help strategy. When we fall into who we are (as if by chance) happiness is evident in the air, and spills over onto everything.

While happiness seems to descend by accident, however, I am sure we can make ourselves accident-prone. Taking in the buoyancy of this poem can help us be more susceptible to it. Seeing the possibility of happiness, distinguishing it from the contentment of material comfort, and also from the excitement, the exuberance, of the high points in our lives—this can make it more likely to strike us.

For if you are anything like me, you may be more eager to identify with the intense moments in your life, the highs and the lows of exhilaration or deep sorrow, rather than with the subtler, quieter current of happiness that can hum along unnoticed. Happiness doesn't need anything to be happening. It is so simple it can be overlooked, especially since it need not be related to external circumstances. And especially since we live in a culture that values intensity, specialness, and personal power above all else. There is nothing more ordinary than sitting in a train, but that moment on the way down to the South of France, some forty years ago, is still alive in me today. Yet there was no action making me unique or special in that moment, simply France passing by.

What is happening when you are happy, then, is *you*. Who you are is happiness, and when you are who you are you are naturally happy. This, surely, is what this poem is beckoning us to: to the weightless freedom at our core.

8

THE GOD ABANDONS ANTONY

by C. P. Cavafy

*When suddenly, at midnight, you hear
an invisible procession going by
with exquisite music, voices,
don't mourn your luck that's failing now,
work gone wrong, your plans
all proving deceptive—don't mourn them uselessly.
As one long prepared, and graced with courage,
say goodbye to her, the Alexandria that is leaving.
Above all, don't fool yourself, don't say
it was a dream, your ears deceived you:
don't degrade yourself with empty hopes like these.
As one long prepared, and graced with courage,
as is right for you who were given this kind of city,
go firmly to the window
And listen with deep emotion, but not
with whining, the pleas of a coward;*

listen—your final delectation—to the voices,
to the exquisite music of that strange procession,
and say goodbye to her, to the Alexandria you are losing.

Don't Mourn Your Luck

In "The God Abandons Antony," C. P. Cavafy wants us to feel, through Antony, the hero of the poem, the experience of losing what is most precious to us, without giving any thought to what might happen next. Can we stand to gaze into the heart of our loss, and not look away?

This is one of Cavafy's most famous poems, and he wrote it in 1911. He draws on the story by Plutarch in which Mark Antony, lover of Cleopatra and ruler of the Eastern Roman Empire, is besieged in Alexandria by Octavian, ruler of the Western Roman Empire. Octavian was intent on consolidating all power into his own hands. In Plutarch's version, the night before the city falls, Mark Antony hears an invisible troupe of musicians and singers leaving the city. At that moment, he passes out, in the realization that the god Bacchus, his protector, and god of music, wine, and festivity, is deserting him; and that he, Antony, is destined to lose the city. Historically, Antony and Cleopatra, on realizing that all is lost, are said to have committed suicide rather than suffer defeat.

Out of this tale, Cavafy fashions his own poetic tour de

force in colloquial Greek, one of the first times that the ver-
nacular, rather than the classical form of the Greek lan-
guage, is used in poetry. It is one of those great poems to
have reached across time and cultural divides to an inter-
national readership because, from the raw historical mate-
rial, Cavafy manages to capture the essence of a human
predicament that every one of us is likely to face at some time
or another—the loss of someone or something that has been
so dear to us we can barely imagine our life without it. Yet the
poem's moral power of character stems from something
deeper still, for Cavafy is urging a special kind of response to
such a loss; a response that calls on our deepest human
reserves of dignity and courage.

C. P. Cavafy knew Alexandria, in Egypt, intimately. He was
born there, of Greek parents in 1863, and though he spent
several of his adolescent years in England, the rest of his life
took place without great incident in his native city. For
Cavafy, as for some of his contemporaries, including the
English authors Lawrence Durrell and E. M. Forster (it was
they who introduced Cavafy's work to an international audi-
ence), Alexandria was alive simultaneously on different myth-
ological and historical layers. It was, especially for Cavafy, a
city of the mind as well as a physical environment.

In Cavafy's imagination, the ancient inhabitants of the city
were as alive in his time as they were in their own. He would
gossip freely with visitors about historical characters and
their scandalous intrigues as if they were just then passing
down the street below his second-floor balcony. In his poetic
works he would often superimpose classical events on con-

temporary affairs or on the events of his own life. There was no shortage of material. In classical times, Alexandria was one of the greatest cities on earth, where people of many faiths and races—Greeks, Romans, Egyptians, Jews, Christians—lived side by side and engaged in a constant creative exchange. The Alexandria of Cavafy's later years was a similar creative milieu that drew artists and writers from around the world.

On reading the first line of "The God Abandons Antony," I paused to wonder why Cavafy has Antony hear the invisible procession at midnight. Perhaps, in those moments when we are alone, and especially at night, we are more receptive to the deeper currents of our life, and to the fuller implications of what it is we might be losing. In the light of day, other business presses in on us, and we can distract ourselves from the starker issues before us. We can appear to push on regardless, in denial. But, as Theodore Roethke says in the first line of his poem "The Taste of Self,"

In a dark time, the eye begins to see.[1]

In the dark of the night, Antony cannot escape what his ears are telling him, that he is in the process of losing something "exquisite." When that happens in a life, it can seem as if even our personal deity, our very life force, is abandoning us, like the wind being blown out of our lungs.

How easy it is to blame the fates, to fall into bitterness and cynicism, or to blame oneself and others for such a sorry turn of fortune. It is useless to avoid responsibility by pointing the finger at others. It is equally useless to mutter over your own misinformed decisions, your wrong choices, what you could have done but didn't, what you did do but should not have done. It serves nothing, Cavafy tells us, to curl up in a ball and mourn what might have been.

Easy to say, difficult to do. You need a firm and quiet attention to forgo responses such as these in favor of Cavafy's call to a deeper, truer emotion. The *dark time* mentioned in Roethke's line, the midnight of Cavafy's poem, evoke a night of spiritual desolation, in which the soul feels as if even God has abandoned it. The shadow of death feels near, purpose and meaning have vanished, one's life seems to be an empty nothingness, a *tattered coat upon a stick,* as Yeats put it.[2] This is an existential desolation, and a necessary stage of anyone's journey.

But in my case, when assailed by such feelings of non-being, I have sometimes projected the experience onto the person dearest to me, my wife, and complained that she is the one causing my trouble, that she is not loving nor warm enough toward me. The truer course would be to accept the gap, the emptiness, at the heart of my own life, and to allow the experience itself to enter me fully, without explanations or rationalizations—to feel all meaning, the light of my life, leaving me, and to watch it float away, as Cavafy urges Antony to do. Then, what happens next will come *with its own heave and grace,* as Mary Oliver says.[3]

Cavafy wants Antony neither to put a brave face on his feelings, nor to indulge them through some form of exaggerated acting out. No, he is calling upon Antony to experience the full weight of his feelings, to be willing to hear the exquisite music and to stand there at the balcony with the courage to acknowledge his loss, to say good-bye to the beauty that he has known, and that is now leaving. You can experience the true weight of loss, the full significance of it, he is saying, only if you have the nobility of soul—the courage—to meet it head on, exactly for what it is, without the protective layer of your own justifications and excuses, or the indulgence in your own mourning. Courage like this can indeed set you free.

In recent years, there has been a chorus of wise voices raising the possibility of the capacity for true feeling that Cavafy is describing here. The author and monk Brother David Steindl-Rast speaks, for example, of the difference between *suffering with life and suffering against life.* To suffer *against life,* he says, is to superimpose a layer of self-conscious suffering on the natural pain (or pleasure) that life offers us. It is to *mourn your luck that's failing now,* as Cavafy says. To *suffer with life,* on the other hand, is to *go firmly to the window* and face the music, so to speak, of the loss of your dream.

> *Above all, don't fool yourself, don't say*
> *it was a dream, your ears deceived you:*
> *don't degrade yourself with empty hopes like these.*

A friend of mine who is selling her house, the one she has lived and loved and worked in for twenty years, told me recently that this is precisely what she has found herself doing. She has noticed herself minimizing the joy and the nourishment she has had in her home, playing down the way it had provided a safe context for many of the most significant moments of her life. She was beginning to realize, she went on, that she had followed the same pattern in relationships. When a relationship ended, she avoided acknowledging the ways it had enriched her life with love. She emphasized instead the benefits of leaving it. Avoiding the beauty of what she was losing seemed to enable her more easily to accept its passing. In reality, she said, she had been protecting herself from the depth of her own love, and denying herself the true poignancy and richness of her own life experience.

Cavafy is fierce in these few lines quoted above: He tells Antony that such a response would only degrade him by disguising his true nobility. Then, in another layer of meaning, he is also warning Antony not to fool himself into thinking that this midnight vision is only a dream, that none of it is happening: that the God isn't leaving after all, and he's not losing Alexandria. Denial is one of our first defenses against change.

> *As one long prepared, and graced with courage,*
> *as is right for you who were given this kind of city,*
> *go firmly to the window*
> *And listen with deep emotion,*

Mark Antony had shown ample courage throughout his life, and was hardly a stranger to loss. He had been a leader in many battles and wars, and had lost much of his reputation and honor because of his marriage to Cleopatra. His was a life that had given him a long preparation in learning to say good-bye. He was worthy of being the lord of Alexandria, jewel of the Orient. And yet even he, it seems, needed the poet's words to give him the resolve to rise to this most difficult of tasks, the full acceptance of the loss of his city, which also implied the loss of his love, Cleopatra, the loss of his position, and ultimately, the loss of his life. Cavafy urges him to go to the window, not to shield himself in any way from what is happening, and to *listen with deep emotion.*

Deep emotion does not need acting out, but it does need the willingness to allow it into your bloodstream, to let its fire fan out from the heart and find its way into the cells of the body. It spans, too, the whole spectrum of human feelings: For notice that the poet calls Antony to his *final delectation*— he challenges him to be so open that he is even able to drink in this last deep pleasure of the music, knowing that he will hear it no more.

At least one contemporary singer and poet has been inspired by Cavafy's poem to write his own song of loss, "Alexandra Leaving." It is one of Leonard Cohen's *Ten New Songs,* the album which came out in 2001. Perhaps it was the loss of a lover that inspired Cohen to write his own version of Cavafy's poem. Or, knowing of his years in a monastery, perhaps it was the loss of the spiritual Beloved.

In the twilight of my own previous relationship, my partner and I invited a small group of dear friends to our house one evening. We wanted to acknowledge in their presence how much we had loved each other, and how grateful we were to have been able to share our life together with them on so many different occasions. We told them this, we told them how much we continued to value and honor each other; and we told them that, after fourteen years, we knew that our lives were taking us in different directions, that we needed to part, despite all the love and companionship we had known. That is the closest I have come in my own life to Mark Antony in Cavafy's poem, standing at the window listening to the departing joy of his life. What that evening did for me was to bring to the forefront my love for my partner, instead of obscuring it with all the reasons that we were leaving each other. In effect, I knew then—I felt then—that there *was* no reason, other than the inevitable procession of a life. That evening stood in clear contrast to the many other times that I had hidden, as Leonard Cohen sings, "behind the cause and the effect."

To listen to the course of our life, to accept it with *deep emotion,* instead of trying to bargain with God, with our lover, even our enemy—and instead of trying to follow the currently fashionable idea of creating a reality of our own choosing—to listen in this way is to keep the embers of our life burning even in our darkest winter. Mark Antony, in Cavafy's poem, is called in this way to his essential dignity. May we, too, have the strength of character to say good-bye to that which is leaving us, and to open our arms to the great unknown that always follows.

9

THANK YOU, MY FATE

by Anna Swir

Great humility fills me,
great purity fills me,
I make love with my dear
as if I made love dying
as if I made love praying,
tears pour
over my arms and his arms.
I don't know whether this is joy
or sadness, I don't understand
what I feel, I'm crying,
I'm crying, it's humility
as if I were dead,
gratitude, I thank you, my fate,
I'm unworthy, how beautiful
my life.

Pure Sex

How can I add even a word to the upwelling of ecstasy that was shaped into the lines of Anna Swir's poem? Her lines carry me away to the far shore of the known I can only float, backtrack, *ramble my way home*[1] without any sure compass beyond the gratitude she offers up at the end of her poem.

Anna Swir, you and your translators from the Polish, Czeslaw Milosz and Leonard Nathan, open a door to the possible with this poem. You make possible with your words what would otherwise be unsayable and therefore beyond what I might ever have known. You pour your passion onto the page, my eyes pass over the words, your rapture rises to meet me. You are a spell maker. Incantations fall from your pen and seize readers like me who would never, could never, have never, thought of love-making in quite this way, all humility, purity, and tears.

> *I am astonished*
> *up to my nostrils . . .*[2]

you say elsewhere, and so too am I with this, one of the finest of your magnificent love poems.

Swir knows that erotic passion, like all passion, has its source not in overwhelming sensations but in something deeper, the soul. This is one of the most ecstatic and erotic love poems you will ever read, but there is no mention of stimulation, arousal, foreplay, or orgasm. Not that any of these aren't marvelous; nor that they didn't take place at the time; but Swir chooses instead to describe her feelings, rather than her sensations. As if the physical love-making took place within the larger field of felt intimacy with her partner. The realm of the soul is that of relatedness, of a genuine connection between people that reaches under the skin.

And yet Swir goes further even than this. She mentions her partner only once in the poem, and then only in a passing remark about her tears falling on his arm. The erotic engages us deeply, she is saying, not just with our partner, but also with ourselves. It is with her own self, and the mystery of what lies beyond form altogether, that she becomes intimate in this poem. This is why the erotic can make us vulnerable. This is the primordial openness that has spilled over and onto the page in the form of Swir's poem.

By contrast, sensation alone—however orgasmic—ultimately fails to deliver the goods. It runs the risk of being only skin deep; its effects are immediate and short-term, and unlike the erotic, sensation lets us off lightly. There is nothing to give, except the cost of the ride. To skim the surface of life, however, is likely to leave us on our own, and ultimately, lonely.

The genuinely erotic, such as Swir pays homage to in this poem, does not let us off lightly precisely because we are laid bare in it. An erotic response to life engages and opens both body and soul. The soul feels deeply, sometimes almost unbearably, the poignancy of life; the body shudders, quivers, trembles with pleasure or sadness—in love-making, while watching the night sky, hearing a Bach chorale, or reading a poem like this one.

> *Great humility fills me,*
> *great purity fills me,*

You may wonder what humility and purity have to do with the erotic. But notice the verb in each of the first two lines— she is filled to overflowing with these *great* feelings, stirred to the core by them, so much so that her love-making seems as if it might be her last act here on earth. Death, more than anything else, obliges us to be real, and the purity she speaks of suggests to me a condition shorn of all artifice; a state in which she is returned to her essence in the company of her lover. There is something about that kind of love-making, the kind in which we are revealed in our truest light, that is immaculate, truly virginal, though not in some other-worldly, anti-sensual way. On the contrary, Swir pairs the word *purity* with *humility*, and *humility* has its roots in *humus*, earth, and is connected to *humor* as well as *human*. Humility, like humor, happens when we are brought down to earth, down into our body, and returned to our senses, rather than removed from them.

> *You gave me rapture,*
> *I gave you rapture.*

Immaculate both
we stare at each other . . .

she says in another of her poems, "Viscera Flicker."[3]

There's something, too, in the bones of "Thank You, My Fate," that brings its erotic power flooding through the lines. See how words and phrases are repeated, one line echoing the previous one, the intensity, the rhythm, rising incrementally. And the short lines, breathless, blown away, at a loss for words—and yet how eloquently they convey her astonishment!

as if I made love dying
as if I made love praying,

What can she mean, as if she were dying, as if she were praying? There have been times when I have made love with my love in such a way as to leave a sad taste in the air—too hurried, too anxious, ambivalent, or sleepy. No tantric explosions, no glorious tsunamis, either sensual or spiritual; occasionally, not even a deep or engaging intimacy. Instead, barely more than a few minutes of flurried activity and then a roll over and good night. How great our possibilities, how small our lives! But then, I remember Rumi:

We're groggy, but let the guilt go.
Feel the motions of tenderness
around you, the buoyancy.[4]

And I remember how many times there have been when, in sheer awe and gratitude, I have staggered to the end of the bed and kissed her feet; when we have been raised up in our love-making to a vulnerability, an openness, that has let the sky pour in. In those moments beyond time our bodies and souls are in service to something beyond ourselves. Perhaps it is simply Life itself. Those moments are love-making as prayer, but it is not I, not we, who do the praying. Rather, the force of life takes over, and we are the ones, it seems, who are acted upon; who are being prayed. Dying, praying: These, too, are meetings—love-makings, if you will—with what is both in and beyond these fragile human forms and psyches. And the physical act of love-making can take us there.

> *I don't know whether this is joy*
> *or sadness, I don't understand*
> *what I feel, . . .*

Isn't that a strange thing, the way joy and sadness edge up so close to each other in love-making that it becomes hard to tell them apart? It is difficult to understand what we feel in moments of ecstasy precisely because our ecstasies take us beyond words and distinctions to the unspeakable that only poetry can begin to give voice to. Then, where do those tears come from if not from a deep underground stream that rarely sees the light of day except in moments like this of rapture?

> *You kiss my tears*
> *and my lips.*

> *You tremble, we both tremble,*
> *we are pierced*
> *by bliss, the suffering of love . . .*

Anna Swir cries in another of her love poems, "Head Down."[5] The tears, she says, come from being pierced by bliss; they tumble out of *the suffering of love.* The word *passion* derives from the Latin *passio,* which means suffering, in the sense of being acted upon. Love acts on us, and we are moved to tears. The suffering implicit in the Latin also means to allow, as in Christ's words, "Suffer the little children to come unto me."[6] We open ourselves to the pain of love, to each other's suffering; we allow ourselves to be revealed—this is the depth of passion Swir is calling forth in this poem.

Neither are these depths for the young only. Anna Swir begins another of her love poems, "The Greatest Love," like this:

> *She is sixty. She lives*
> *the greatest love of her life.*[7]

As for me, I am no more than a year from that sober milestone, and only now am I, too, living that great love.

> *gratitude, I thank you, my fate,*
> *I'm unworthy, how beautiful*
> *my life.*

These lines, in perfect rhythm and harmony, capture some of the most beautiful sentiments we can know. After love-making—after or during anything, but especially, perhaps, love-making—gratitude comes. Gratitude for the love itself, but more than that, for the fate we have been given, which has allowed us to know an experience like this, even if only once in our lives. How often do we give thanks for our fate? And then, to feel the wonder of the gift, the gift of your own unique life, so profoundly that you feel unworthy of all its beauty? What an astonishing grace, to be able to know the heartbreaking happiness of being alive in this body of clay.

10

IN SILENCE

by Thomas Merton

Be still
Listen to the stones of the wall.
Be silent, they try
To speak your

Name.
Listen
To the living walls.
Who are you?
Who
Are you? Whose
Silence are you?

Who (be quiet)
Are you (as these stones
Are quiet). Do not
Think of what you are
Still less of

What you may one day be.
Rather
Be what you are (but who?) be
The unthinkable one
You do not know.

O be still, while
You are still alive,
And all things live around you
Speaking (I do not hear)
To your own being,
Speaking by the Unknown
That is in you and in themselves.

"I will try, like them
To be my own silence:
And this is difficult. The whole
World is secretly on fire. The stones
Burn, even the stones
They burn me. How can a man be still or
Listen to all things burning? How can he dare
To sit with them when
All their silence
Is on fire?"

The Whole World, Secretly on Fire

In the early 1960s, Thomas Merton was one of the first Christian monks to take an active interest in the spiritual traditions of the East. He was especially drawn to Buddhism because of its profound understanding of the human mind, and its placing of spirituality in the recesses of the human heart, rather than in outer forms and rituals. For Merton stands in the long line of those Christian mystics, from Meister Eckhart to John of the Cross, for whom the true God, who is within all things, can be approached only by the heart's intuition. Merton would have echoed the words of John of the Cross in his poem "The Dark Night,"

> *I had no light or guide*
> *But the fire that burned inside my chest.*[1]

Merton was not only a monk but also a prolific, bestselling author and a gifted poet. In this extraordinary poem, "In Silence," Merton tells us that even the stones speak, that they know who we are, and that they will tell us if we can be still enough to hear them. The universe, then, is alive with an intelligence that mirrors the light of knowledge that lives in us. Not the information in our frontal lobes, but the intelligence of the heart's deep core. If we can be still enough— and that *if* is everything—Merton says we might hear the stones speak our own true Name. The name that is ours with a capital *N*. I am reminded of the passage by Franz Kafka, where he says that

> You need not leave your room. Remain seated at your table and listen. You need not even listen; simply wait. You need not even wait; just be quiet, still, and solitary. The world will freely offer itself to you to be unmasked. It has no choice; it will roll in ecstasy at your feet.[2]

And this haiku poem by the Chinese poet Do Hyun Choe:

> *Stillness is what creates love.*
> *Movement is what creates life.*
> *To be still*
> *And still moving—*
> *That is everything.*[3]

Merton uses the verb *listen* twice in the first six short lines, just as Kafka does in his few lines of prose. There is something in the quality of listening that can lead us to the stillness he is encouraging us to be. When we listen to the life in the world about us with an active, relaxed attentiveness, we allow our self-consciousness, the observer in us, to fade away.

Deep listening—whether to the stones in the wall of our house, to the birdsong outside, or to our companion across the kitchen table—joins us to the living world. It melts the judging mind, it softens the separation between our own consciousness and that of life itself. That softening is true relaxation, the release of the tensions in the cells of the body; and with that relaxation of body as well as of mind, stillness arises.

Notice how Merton encourages this listening by means of his poem's structure. The short lines—often just a single word—leave a great deal of space on the page, so that the words themselves seem to rise up out of a deep white silence. And the one or two word lines slow down the reading. Your eye is shaken from its usual custom of following the line from one side of the page to the other, and has to dwell for a moment on each of the individual words—

> *Be still*
> . . . .
> *Name.*
> *Listen*
> . . . .
> *Who*

The deepest stillness I have ever known was in a cave on Arunachala Hill, in southern India.[4] The cave used to be the home of the Indian saint Ramana Maharshi. At the cave entrance is a little courtyard, with a single breadfruit tree that shades a lingam—the phallic stone that represents the source of creation for Hindus—set in a circle of water. Someone had left a red rose on the lingam head. I sat on the low parapet that skirted the tree, and gazed down onto the city of Tiruvannamalai below me. Even though traffic horns boomed right up the mountain, the courtyard was unusually tranquil.

I took off my shoes and passed through a vestibule hung with pictures of Ramana into the darkness of the cave itself. Three people were sitting motionless in front of a stone ledge. I sat down on the floor near them. The air was hot and thick. The silence and the stillness began to enter my mind.

What a relief it was, to be in the darkness after the glare of the south Indian sun. I sensed the wisdom of those builders of old Romanesque churches, which in Europe I had so often passed by in favor of the radiance and soaring of their Gothic successors. This cave, like one of those early churches, was a womb. Its darkness was the darkness of not knowing, of some secret germination beyond the aspirations or grasp of the daylight mind. Maybe I was there for an hour or so, when out of nowhere a voice suddenly rang through the quiet of my body: *Just rest,* it said. *Just rest.*

I had thought I was already at rest, but as I heard these words I was instantly aware of the subtle effort I had been making all along to be aware of the silence I was in. Even that effort was a residual holding back from being there, where I was, in utter simplicity. I let the dark cave take me then, hold me; and in that moment it was as if the mountain moved through me. It seemed in that moment that the life of the mountain, the cave, and my own innermost being were one and the same thing.

This, I think, is what Merton is speaking to here in this poem. In this depth of silence, the question *Who are you?* is likely to emerge naturally, as if the silence itself is asking the question. The only spiritual practice that Ramana Maharshi recommended to the thousands of people who came to him from all over India, and indeed, the world, was the asking of this question.

> *Who (be quiet)*
> *Are you (as these stones*
> *Are quiet). Do not*
> *Think of what you are*
> *Still less of*
> *What you may one day be.*
> *Rather*
> *Be what you are (but who?) be*
> *The unthinkable one*
> *You do not know.*

This is exactly as Ramana advised. Do not ask the question with the thinking mind, expecting a thought for an answer. It is not a matter of answers, but of falling deeply into the question itself, of *being* the question. That is easy to say, difficult to do. Perhaps you already know that your true identity can never be described by your personal attributes, or by what you do in the world. Answers to Merton's question *Who are you?* like, "I am a mother, a company director, a writer, an actor, a musician," rise only from our surface.

Perhaps, then, a deeper response might be something like

this: "I am pure peace, I am love, a unique expression of the spirit in form, a soul on its own unique journey." But no. To answer this way is still to remain at the level of concepts. Merton, in his poem, and Ramana Maharshi, in his teachings, want to coax us beyond concepts altogether. Can we dare to hold the question, to feel the force that the words contain, without leaping to diffuse its potency with a clever answer? As we rest deeper and deeper into the silence that is at the heart of everything, we are able to rest in who we are beyond all thought and reason. We are able to be the one we do not know. This is the greatest freedom available to us as human beings.

I love what the Chinese poet says, in the haiku poem quoted earlier, that stillness is what creates love. For if we can be still enough in life (instead of waiting until death) to see the life in all things, we will see with the eyes of love. You will see that all things are

> *Speaking (I do not hear)*
> *To your own being,*
> *Speaking by the Unknown*
> *That is in you and in themselves.*

Things speak, not of themselves, but by and through the Unknown that is in all things. In stillness, we fall into the Unknown in ourselves, and the world comes alive in a whole new way. We see that the world is on fire, burning with life, with a passion for existence that is invisible to our ordinary eyes.

How can a man be still or
Listen to all things burning? How can he dare
To sit with them when
All their silence
Is on fire?

Merton knows of what he speaks. He was a mystic, remember, who spent much of his time in solitude in a small hut on the grounds of the Abbey of Gethsemani, in Kentucky. The only way you can *Listen to all things burning* is to let go of who you think you are and fall into the stillness in which your familiar name is burned to ashes. Do I know what he means when he says that all things are burning? In this moment, no. This kind of knowing—this kind of burning—is not something that can be retrieved from memory. It is a wholehearted devotion that has to be lived in the present moment or not at all. And his question to you and to me is, Do we dare sit in this silence now, and risk everything we know going up in smoke? For this is the fire that will set us free; free to know who we truly are.

About the Poets

DAVID WHYTE (b.1955) was born and raised in the north of England, studied marine zoology in Wales, and trained as a naturalist in the Galápagos Islands. He now lives in the Pacific Northwest with his wife and two children, and works full-time as a poet, reading and lecturing throughout the world. He is one of the few poets to bring his insights to bear on organizational life, working with corporations at home and abroad. He has published four volumes of poetry, and has also written two best-selling prose books.

JANE HIRSHFIELD (b.1953) is a prize-winning poet, translator, editor, and author of five collections of poetry. *Given Sugar, Given Salt* was a finalist for the National Book Critics Circle Award in 2001. Her work addresses the life of the passions, the way the objects and events of everyday life are informed by deeper wisdoms and by the darkness and losses of life. Her poetry searches continually for the point where new knowledge of the world and self may appear, and carries the influence of her lifelong study and practice of Buddhism. Originally from New York City, she has lived in the Bay Area for many years.

MIGUEL DE UNAMUNO (1864–1936) was a Basque from Bilbao, one of ten children of a grocer. He went on to learn fourteen languages, to hold various university chairs in Spain, and to be the rector of the University of Salamanca. A predecessor of the Existentialists, his philosophical essays had great influence in early-twentieth-century Spain. He wrote nearly all of his poetry in the last eight years of his life, and was later to be an important influence on the two great Spanish poets Juan Ramón Jiménez and Antonio Machado. His liberal political views frequently caused him to be exiled, and ultimately brought about his death, a few months into the Spanish Civil War, when he denounced Franco and fascism.

RUMI (1207–1273) was the founder of the Sufi order known as the Mevlevi (Whirling Dervishes) in Konya, Turkey. Though the theme of lover and beloved was already established in Sufi teaching, his own poetry was inspired by his meeting and the consequent loss of his great teacher, Shams of Tabriz. Out of their relationship was born some of the most inspired love poetry ever, in which Rumi sings of a love that is both personal and divine at the same time. After Shams's death, Rumi would burst into ecstatic poetry anywhere, anytime, and his scribe and disciple, Husam, was charged with writing it all down. Rumi's great spiritual treatise, *The Mathnawi,* written in couplets, amounts to more than twenty-five thousand lines in six books.

MARY OLIVER (b.1935) is one of America's most widely read contemporary poets. The critic Alice Ostriker contends that Oliver is "as visionary as Emerson." She won her first poetry prize at the age of twenty-seven, from the Poetry Society of America, for her collection *No Voyage.* She won the Pulitzer prize in 1984 for her collection of poems, *American Primitive,* and she was winner of the 1992 National Book Award for poetry for her *New and Selected Poems.* In an interview for the *Bloomsbury Review* in 1990, she said, "I feel that the function of the poet is to be . . . somehow instructive and opinionated, useful even if only as a devil's advocate. . . . The question asked today is: What does it mean? Nobody says, 'How does it feel?' "

STANLEY KUNITZ (b.1905) worked for many years as an editor in New York City before achieving major recognition for his poetry, which came with a Pulitzer prize in 1958 for his *Collected Poems.* Since then, he has won many prizes and honors. In 2000 he was the U.S. Poet Laureate, and in 1995 his collection *Passing Through* won the National Book Award. He taught for many years in the graduate writing program at Columbia, and continues to live in Manhattan and also in Provincetown, Massachusetts. His more recent poems combine a quiet restraint with a deep current of passion. Now well into his nineties, he continues to write actively.

NAOMI SHIHAB NYE (b.1952) was born of a Palestinian father and an American mother. Her work consistently reveals the poignancy and the paradoxes that emerge from feeling an intimate relationship with two different cultures. Raised in St. Louis, Missouri, she has lived in Jerusalem, and now resides with her family in San Antonio, Texas. Her poems and short stories have appeared in reviews and magazines all over the world. Besides her six volumes of poetry, she has also written books for children and edited several anthologies of prose. She first started writing poetry at the age of six. "Somehow, I knew what a poem was. I liked the comfortable, portable shape of poems . . . and especially the way they took you to a deeper, quieter place, almost immediately."

CONSTANTINE P. CAVAFY (1863–1933) was the most original and influential Greek poet of the twentieth century, though close to a third of his poems were never printed in any form until after his death. He lived most of his life in Alexandria, Egypt, though his family moved to England for seven years when he was nine, and from there went to Istanbul for two more years before returning to a life of genteel poverty in Alexandria. Cavafy, who was homosexual, lived with his mother until her death in 1899, and then with his unmarried brothers. He worked for thirty years as a government clerk in the Ministry of Public Works in Egypt. He had a twenty-year acquaintance with the English writer E. M. Forster.

ANNA SWIR (1900–1984) was the only daughter of an impoverished artist, and grew up in his studio in Warsaw, Poland. A militant feminist and author of uninhibited love poems, her work conveys an erotic intensity and warmth, along with an empathy and compassion for those who suffer. Her poems on war and the Nazi occupation of Poland were among the finest of her generation. Czeslaw Milosz and Leonard Nathan have translated her work into English.

THOMAS MERTON (1915–1968) was a Trappist monk, poet, and peace activist. In 1947, his autobiography, *The Seven Storey Mountain,* was a surprise best-seller, and profoundly influenced the immediate postwar interest in monasticism and religion. In the sixties, he became one of the first authoritative Christian voices to take a serious interest in Eastern spirituality, especially Buddhism. He translated Buddhist poets, and in 1968 attended an interfaith meeting of monastic superiors in Bangkok. On that same journey, he met the Dalai Lama in India, and they recognized each other as kindred spirits. Tragically, Merton was electrocuted accidentally in his Bangkok hotel room, and died there.

Notes

INTRODUCTION

1. Excerpt from "The Journey" by Mary Oliver. In *New and Selected Poems*. Boston: Beacon Press, 1992.

1 "SELF-PORTRAIT"

1. Excerpt from "Sweet Darkness" by David Whyte. In *The House of Belonging*. Langley, Wash.: Many Rivers Press, 1997.
2. Excerpt from "What I Must Tell Myself" by David Whyte. In *The House of Belonging*.
3. Excerpt from "The Road Not Taken" by Robert Frost. In *The Poetry of Robert Frost: The Collected Poems*. Ed. Edward C. Latham. New York: Henry Holt, 1987.
4. Excerpt from "The Man Watching" by Rainer Maria Rilke. In *Selected Poems of Rainer Maria Rilke*. Trans. Robert Bly. New York: Harper & Row, 1981.

2 "LAKE AND MAPLE"

1. Excerpt from "A Prayer for Old Age" by W. B. Yeats. In *The Collected Poems of W. B. Yeats*. Ed. Richard J. Finneran. New York: Scribner, 2nd revised edition, 1996.
2. Excerpt from "Have You Ever Tried to Enter the Long Black Branches?" by Mary Oliver. In this book and in *West Wind: Poems and Prose Poems*. Boston: Houghton Mifflin, 1997.
3. Excerpt from "Ripeness" by Jane Hirshfield. In *The October Palace*. New York: HarperCollins, 1994.
4. Psalm 46:10.
5. Extract from "There Is a Passion in Me" by Rumi. In *Like This: 43 Odes*, Versions by Coleman Barks. Athens, Ga.: Maypop Books, 1990.
6. Excerpt from *Hsin-Hsin Ming: Verses on the Faith Mind* by Seng-ts'an. 606 AD. Trans. Richard B. Clark. Buffalo, N.Y.: White Pine Press, 2001.

3 "THROW YOURSELF LIKE SEED"

1. Excerpt from *Temenidæ*. Frag. 734, Euripides.

2. Excerpt from "Wild Geese" by Mary Oliver. In *New and Selected Poems.* Boston: Beacon Press, 1992.

3. Excerpt from "The Man Watching" by Rainer Maria Rilke. In *Selected Poems of Rainer Maria Rilke.* Trans. Robert Bly. New York: Harper & Row, 1981.

4. Extract from *The Scottish Himalaya Expedition* by W. H. Murray. London: J. M. Dent & Son, 1951 (out of print).

4   "UNFOLD YOUR OWN MYTH"

1. G. I. Gurdjieff, *Meetings with Remarkable Men.* New York: E. P. Dutton, 1991.

2. Excerpt from "Wilderness" by Laurens van der Post in *Lapis* magazine, issue 2. The article was edited from "Wilderness," a talk given by Sir Laurens van der Post in London in 1995 at the inauguration of the Wilderness Trust in Great Britain.

3. James Hillman, *The Soul's Code: In Search of Character and Calling.* New York: Warner Books, 1997.

4. For more on Nanagaru, and a photo of him, see my book *Travels Through Sacred India.* London, England: Thorsons, 1996.

5. From "Self-Portrait" by David Whyte in this book and in his *Fire in the Earth.* Langley, Wash.: Many Rivers Press, 1992.

5   "HAVE YOU EVER TRIED TO ENTER THE LONG BLACK BRANCHES?"

1. Revelations 3:15–16.

6   "THE LAYERS"

1. Extract from a letter to George and Georgiana Keats, dated February 14, 1819. John Keats wrote: "Call the world if you please 'The Vale of Soul-Making.'" In *Keats: Poems and Selected Letters.* Ed. Carlos Baker. New York: Scribner, 1962.

2. See the opening passage of Comments on the Spiritual Exercises of Ignatius Loyola, in *Gerard Manley Hopkins: Poems and Prose.* New York: Penguin Books, 1985 (". . . when I consider my selfbeing, my consciousness and feelings of myself, that taste of myself, of I and *me* above and in all things, which is much more distinctive than the taste of ale or alum. . . . and is incommunicable by any means to another man").

3. See *What the Living Do: Poems* by Marie Howe. Three of her poems are also in my anthology *Risking Everything: 110 Poems of Love and Revelation.* New York: Harmony Books, 2003.

7   "SO MUCH HAPPINESS"

1. Extract from a letter to John Taylor from John Keats, dated February 27, 1818. In *Keats: Poems and Selected Letters.* Ed. Carlos Baker. New York: Scribner, 1962.
2. Carol Shields, *Unless: A Novel.* New York: Fourth Estate, 2002.
3. Alain de Botton, *The Art of Travel.* New York: Pantheon, 2002.
4. Extract from *Song of Myself* by Walt Whitman, 1885 ed.

8   "THE GOD ABANDONS ANTONY"

1. Extract from "The Taste of Self" by Theodore Roethke. In *The Collected Poems of Theodore Roethke.* New York: Anchor Books, 1975.
2. Extract from "Sailing to Byzantium" by W. B. Yeats. In *The Collected Works of W. B. Yeats.* Ed. Richard J. Finneran. New York: Scribner, 2d revised edition, 1996.

   An aged man is but a paltry thing,
   A tattered coat upon a stick, unless
   Soul clap its hands and sing, and louder sing . . .

3. Extract from "Have You Ever Tried to Enter the Long Black Branches?" by Mary Oliver. In this book and in *West Wind: Poems and Prose Poems.* Boston: Houghton Mifflin, 1997.

9   "THANK YOU, MY FATE"

1. Extract from "Have You Ever Tried to Enter the Long Black Branches?" by Mary Oliver. In this book and in *West Wind: Poems and Prose Poems.* Boston: Houghton Mifflin, 1997.
2. Extract from "Dithyramb of a Happy Woman" by Anna Swir. In *Happy as a Dog's Tail.* Trans. Czeslaw Milosz. New York: Harcourt Brace, 1985.
3. Extract from "Viscera Flicker" by Anna Swir. In *Happy as a Dog's Tail.*
4. Extract from "Buoyancy" by Rumi. In *The Essential Rumi.* Trans. Coleman Barks with John Moyne. San Francisco: HarperSanFrancisco, 1995.
5. Extract from "Head Down" by Anna Swir. In *Happy as a Dog's Tail.*

6. Mark 10:14.
7. Extract from "The Greatest Love" by Anna Swir. In *Talking to My Body*. Trans. Czeslaw Milosz and Leonard Nathan. Port Townsend, Washington: Copper Canyon Press, 1996.

10 "IN SILENCE"

1. Extract from "The Dark Night" by John of the Cross. In *The Soul Is Here for Its Own Joy*. Ed. and trans. Robert Bly. New York: Ecco Press, 1995.
2. Extract from *The Great Wall of China and Other Stories* by Franz Kafka. London, England: Penguin, 1991.
3. I cannot trace the source of this poem.
4. For more on Ramana Maharshi and my visit to Arunachala, see my book *Travels Through Sacred India*. London, England: Thorsons, 1996.

Recommended Reading

DAVID WHYTE

Fire in the Earth
Where Many Rivers Meet
The House of Belonging
Crossing the Unknown Sea: Work as a Pilgrimage of Identity (nonfiction)

JANE HIRSHFIELD

The October Palace
The Lives of the Heart
Given Sugar, Given Salt

MIGUEL DE UNAMUNO

Unamuno's poetry is not available in English, though there are several Spanish versions. The poem "Throw Yourself Like Seed" was translated by Robert Bly and appeared in *Roots and Wings: Poetry from Spain 1900–1975*, edited by Hardie St. Martin, 1976, now out of print.

RUMI

The Essential Rumi. Trans. Coleman Barks with John Moyne
The Soul of Rumi. Trans. Coleman Barks
Love's Glory: Re-Creations of Rumi. Trans. Andrew Harvey

MARY OLIVER

Read anything you can get your hands on, but especially
New and Selected Poems
The Leaf and the Cloud
West Wind: Poems and Prose Poems
What Do We Know

STANLEY KUNITZ

Passing Through: The Later Poems, New and Selected
The Collected Poems of Stanley Kunitz

NAOMI SHIHAB NYE

Fuel
Words Under the Words: Selected Poems

C. P. CAVAFY

The Complete Poems of Cavafy: An Expanded Edition. Trans. Rae Dalver.

ANNA SWIR

Happy as a Dog's Tail. Trans. Czeslaw Milosz and Leonard Nathan.
Talking to My Body. Trans. Czeslaw Milosz and Leonard Nathan.

THOMAS MERTON

The Collected Poems of Thomas Merton
The Seven Storey Mountain
The Intimate Merton: His Life from His Journals

Further Recommended Reading

ROBERT BLY
Eating the Honey of Words

BILLY COLLINS
Sailing Alone Around the Room: New and Selected Poems
Picnic, Lightning

G. I. GURDJIEFF
Meetings with Remarkable Men

GERARD MANLEY HOPKINS
Gerard Manley Hopkins: Poems and Prose

MARIA HOUSDEN
Hannah's Gift: Lessons from a Life Fully Lived (nonfiction)

ROGER HOUSDEN
Risking Everything: 110 Poems of Love and Revelation (editor)
Ten Poems to Open Your Heart
Ten Poems to Change Your Life

MARIE HOWE
What the Living Do: Poems

ANTONIO MACHADO
Times Alone: Selected Poems of Antonio Machado (Trans. Robert Bly)

CZESLAW MILOSZ
New and Selected Poems 1931–2001
Striving Toward Being: The Letters of Thomas Merton and Czeslaw Milosz

RAINER MARIA RILKE
Letters to a Young Poet (Trans. Stephen Mitchell)
The Selected Poetry of Rainer Maria Rilke (Trans. Stephen Mitchell)

SENG TS'AN, THIRD ZEN PATRIARCH
The Hsin-Hsin Ming: Verses on the Faith Mind (Trans. Richard B. Clark)

WILLIAM WORDSWORTH
Favorite Poems

POETRY ANTHOLOGIES
Staying Alive: Real Poems for Unreal Times (Ed. Neil Astley)
Poems to Live By in Uncertain Times (Ed. Joan Murray)
The Soul Is Here for Its Own Joy (Ed. Robert Bly)
The Enlightened Heart: An Anthology of Sacred Poetry (Ed. Stephen Mitchell)
A Book of Luminous Things (Ed. Czeslaw Milosz)

Acknowledgments

I am indebted first and foremost to the ten poets whose work I include in this book. Then, dear Kim Rosen, once again your help with considering poems for this collection and your editorial advice have served to shape the final work: a thousand thanks. Toinette Lippe, your enthusiasm as my editor, as well as your eagle eye, have been invaluable throughout the process, as has the care and support of Shaye Areheart, whose persistence ensured we came up with the right title. Kim Witherspoon, my agent, thank you for working my corner as hard as you have done.

Permissions

About the Author

Roger Housden, a native of Bath, England, emigrated to the United States in 1998. He now lives in New York City with his wife, Maria. He is the author of several books, all of which explore in different ways the existential and spiritual issues of our time. His most recent works include *Risking Everything: 110 Poems of Love and Revelation, Ten Poems to Open Your Heart, Chasing Rumi: A Fable About Finding the Heart's True Desire,* and *Ten Poems to Change Your Life.* He gives a small number of individual coaching sessions by phone on the transformational power of poetry and on the life themes covered in the Ten Poems series. You can email him at *tenpoems@gmail.com.*

ALSO BY ROGER HOUSDEN

Dancing with Joy
$20.00 hardcover (Canada: $25.00)
978-0-307-34195-2

Ten Poems to Change Your Life
$16.00 hardcover (Canada: $21.00)
978-0-609-60901-9

*Ten Poems to Change Your Life
Again and Again*
$16.95 hardcover (Canada: $21.00)
978-0-307-40519-7

 AVAILABLE WHEREVER BOOKS ARE SOLD.